The Open

Resource
Book

2

Writing
Successful
Essays

This publication forms part of an Open University course LB160 *Professional Communication for Business Studies*. Details of this and other Open University courses can be obtained from the Student Registration and Enquiry Service, The Open University, PO Box 197, Milton Keynes MK7 6BJ, United Kingdom: tel. +44 (0)845 300 60 90, email general-enquiries@open.ac.uk

Alternatively, you may visit the Open University website at www.open.ac.uk where you can learn more about the wide range of courses and packs offered at all levels by The Open University.

To purchase a selection of Open University course materials visit http://www.ouw.co.uk, or contact Open University Worldwide, Michael Young Building, Walton Hall, Milton Keynes MK7 6AA, United Kingdom for a brochure. tel. +44 (0)1908 858793; fax +44 (0)1908 858787; email ouw-customer-services@open.ac.uk

The Open University

Walton Hall, Milton Keynes

MK7 6AA

First published 2008

Edited and designed by The Open University.

Typeset by Pam Callow, S&P Enterprises Ltd.

Printed in the United Kingdom by Martins the Printers, Berwick-upon-Tweed.

ISBN 978 0 7492 1788 4

1.1

FSC

Mixed Sources

Product group from well-managed forests and other controlled sources

Cert no. TT-COC-2200
www.fsc.org
© 1996 Forest Stewardship Council

Contents

Session 1 resources

Extract 1.1

Company overview

'If you have a body, you are an athlete'

Bill Bowerman said this a couple of decades ago. The guy was right. It defines how he viewed the world, and it defines how Nike pursues its destiny. Ours is a language of sports, a universally understood lexicon of passion and competition. A lot has happened at Nike in the years since we entered the industry, most of it good, some of it downright embarrassing. But through it all, we remain totally focused on creating performance opportunities for everyone who would benefit, and offering empowering messages for everyone who would listen.

(Source: http://www.nike.com/nikebiz/nikebiz.jhtml?page=3)

Extract 1.2

The official LBJ IV review Post!!!

These are probably the most comfortable Bball shoes in my collection of hoop shoes. I wore them to practice last night and did a walk through in them. The traction is top notch. They gripped so well for me I thought it could be dangerous to your knees. I was on a dirty floor and out of a possible 5, they get 5 from me. The comfort factor is a 5 as well. I'm so pleased with this shoe, I'm almost lost for the right words.

I did some drills for a bit and tried to keep an open mind about the shoe and deny my delight of having new shoes on and the fact that nobody else had these on. I think after playing many minutes in these, you'll pick up on the weight factor. ...

(Source: shoes.about.com/gi/dynamic/offsite.htm?zi=1/XJ/Ya&sdn=shoes&cdn=style&tm=60&gps=168_815_962_555&f=00&tt=14&bt=1&bts=1&zu=http%3A//niketalk.com/ [accessed 10 September 2007])

Extract 1.3

Explain why Nike is the biggest training shoe company in the world.

For Nike to compete with other brands of training shoe it has developed a marketing strategy to make the Nike brand highly desirable. The technique of communicating an 'image' is paramount in promoting the symbolic status of the goods it is selling. The marketing of the Nike brand draws upon an emotional appeal for the product that indicates individual success, personal achievement and self-fulfilment. The use of the famous 'Just do it' advertising slogan epitomises this marketing technique by intimating, in a vague manner, that with Nike shoes on your feet, anything is possible. ... Nike's advertising campaigns seek to 'shift the selling point away from the product itself and into a world of their own making' (Vanderbilt, 1998, p. 7).

(Source: adapted from OU Business School student assignment)

Extract 1.4

Explain why Nike is the biggest training shoe company in the world.

The training shoe industry is big business today, despite being a fairly new phenomenon, with trainers only being available to the mass market since jogging became a popular activity in the 1970s. The training shoe itself is now more than just for 'sport'. Most people today own a pair of trainers even though their trainers may never go near a running track or sports field. People wear them for fashion and image. If you think of trainers, you will think of Nike. The name is derived from the Greek god of 'victory'. Many famous sports stars wear Nike trainers and make very large amounts of money from sponsorship so Nike shoes are seen all round the world at sports events. Michael Jordan is the second best known person in China, after Mao Tse Tung, thanks to Nike.

(Source: adapted from OU Business School student assignment)

Words which link back to the title	
Words which identify the key concepts in the essay	
Words which state the central argument of the essay	
Words which say how the essay will be organised	

Extract 1.5

Explain why Nike is the biggest training shoe company in the world.

Originally launched by Philip Knight and Bill Bowerman, Nike soon realised that they could not manufacture trainers cheaply within America and so outsourced production, which still happens today ... To ensure quality production a number of specialist people have been placed into these factories and their job is quality control. This ensures that only perfect articles reach consumers, and that Nike's integrity is protected at all times. Recently Nike have, to placate human rights activists, introduced a new vice-president's post for corporate and social responsibility. He ensures that working conditions, age limits, independent monitoring, education, small business finance and research funding all take place; all of which assist the local populace who make the shoes, which in turn increases Nike's image across the world.

(Source: adapted from OU Business School student assignment)

Words which link back to the title	
Words which identify the key concepts in the essay	
Words which state the central argument of the essay	
Words which say how the essay will be organised	

Extract 1.6

Explain why Nike is the biggest training shoe company in the world.

Nike is the biggest training shoe company in the world, clearly dominating a huge international market, with a market share of 43% in the USA and 35% in the UK (Sturges, 2005, p. 11). In this essay I will argue that Nike has achieved this position because of three factors: timely recognition of the nature of the market and its potential; the innovative philosophy and management style of CEO Phil Knight; and an inspired marketing campaign of sustained brilliance laced with good luck. Nike's combined success in these three areas has made the company into a market leader.

(Source: adapted from OU Business School student assignment)

Words which link back to the title	
Words which identify the key concepts in the essay	
Words which state the central argument of the essay	
Words which say how the essay will be organised	

Text 1.7

Explain why Nike is the biggest training shoe company in the world.

For a company to be regarded as *the biggest* in its business sector, it has to be *successful*. Nike is certainly a story of success. From its humble origins in the early 1970s to a 43% market share in the USA, the success of Nike has been built on two strategies: *marketing and innovation*. This essay will examine how the marketing strategy and the company mission 'to bring inspiration and innovation to every athlete in the world' (Nike company website, 2005) have made the company into a leading brand throughout the world.

Nike was launched in the USA in 1972 by Philip Knight, a former university runner with strong business acumen and his university coach, Bill Bowerman. Whilst studying at university Knight's business skills were evident when he produced a paper citing the benefits of producing sports shoes in countries with cheaper labour than the USA (a policy now implemented by all major training shoe companies). The major points of the paper were reduction of manufacturing costs and the concept that the appeal of a shoe was not in where it was made or how it was manufactured, but in the way that it was marketed.

For Nike to compete with other brands of training shoe it has developed a marketing strategy to make the Nike brand highly desirable. The technique of communicating an 'image' is paramount in promoting the symbolic status of the goods it is selling. The marketing of the Nike brand draws upon an emotional appeal for the product that indicates individual success, personal achievement and self-fulfilment. The use of the famous 'Just do it' advertising slogan epitomises this marketing technique by intimating, in a vague manner, that with Nike shoes on your feet, anything is possible. Nike's advertising campaigns seek to 'shift the selling point away from the product itself and into a world of their own making' (Vanderbilt, 1998).

Training shoe companies invest a great deal of money in advertising to promote their products and convey the concept of emotional appeal. According to Sturges, in 1998 Nike spent £10 million on advertising trainers in the UK alone; this was over twice the amount spent by Reebok and five times that spent by Adidas (Sturges, 2005, p. 33). The advertising portrays sporting stars as heroes who are also stylish and fashionable, emitting a message that sport is fashion.

[Paragraph on sports stars omitted]

Another aspect of the Nike marketing strategy is to use the technique of exclusivity to bolster the appeal of the brand. Nike use a method called 'tiered selling' to promote the trainer and create exclusivity. [*Keep on Running*, Open University video] By only releasing a limited number of trainers (i.e. 5000) at the launch of a new design and selling them at carefully selected venues, Nike creates an exclusive 'club' of owners for a period of time until the shoe goes to the market in greater volume. This creates hype at launch and a demand for the product.

Innovation is another tool in the Nike success story, innovation in both business and technological terms. As mentioned previously, the idea of Philip Knight to focus on marketing the trainer rather than manufacturing it is at the heart of Nike's success. The production of a training shoe is labour intensive so shifting manufacturing to countries in South East Asia which had low wage levels, compared to that of the USA, saves costs and increases profitability. Rather than setting up factories in SE Asia, Nike outsourced manufacturing completely to companies in the designated regions, thus reducing the need for capital investment in factories and equipment. This strategy has been criticised as abusing human rights of the workers in factories that offer poor pay and oppressive working conditions. But the company has turned this criticism to its advantage and made corporate responsibility a company priority. A potentially bad situation has been used as another opportunity for innovation and leadership (Nike, 2004, *Corporate Responsibility Report*).

Nike has also been innovative in its design and technology application. The average development of a trainer is 18 months and design is paramount for consumer appeal, as Tom Vanderbilt (1998, p. 66) explained '... design is what makes the product exciting, new and innovative.' Nike has spent enormous amounts of money on research and development and designs of its products. Since 1995 Nike has tripled its design budget and employs over 300 designers (Sturges, 2005, p. 24). Design is crucial to the commercial success of a product, especially in the training shoe market where style and technology combined produce a winning combination. Nike has led the way with technological advances in the training shoe market with developments such as the use of pockets of pressurised gas and waffle sole designs.

So in conclusion, the innovative approach of Nike of reducing overheads by outsourcing manufacturing of the training shoes in countries where labour costs are low, combined with focus on design and marketing has secured Nike the position of biggest training shoe company in the world. Nike has designed its products to be both functional and fashionable to appeal to target markets outside of sport. Successful marketing has created a brand known around the world and the Nike 'Swoosh' logo is instantly recognisable. Sponsorship of carefully selected sporting stars and slick advertising campaigns has promoted the Nike brand effectively. Nike has understood the environment in which to produce quality, affordable products and the market requirements to sell millions of shoes.

(Source: OU Business School student assignment)

Extract 1.8

Explain why Nike is the biggest training shoe company in the world.

[P1] Nike is a brand that a large majority of people are familiar with, but many know less about the history of the company and the impact it has on society. This paper will investigate how Nike developed. The company has grown very rapidly from a small business idea in the University of Oregon. In 1966 Nike opened its first retail outlet in a narrow building at 3107 Pico Blvd in Santa Monica. In the first year they made just $364 and by 1969 sales had risen to a million dollars. Since then it has developed every year.

[P2] Since 1995 Nike has tripled its design budget and employs over 300 designers.

[P3] In 1998 Nike spent £10 million on advertising trainers in the UK alone.

[P4] It is reported that the Nike sponsorship deal with golfer Tiger Woods is worth $90 million.

[P5] By 2004, Nike had 43% market share in the US.

[P6] Close to 1 million people work for Nike.

[P7] So, there can be no doubt that Nike is the biggest training shoe company in the world.

(Source: OU Business School student assignment)

Extract 1.9

Innovation is another tool in the **Nike success story**, innovation in both **business and technological terms**. As mentioned previously, the idea of Philip Knight to focus on marketing the trainer rather than manufacturing it is at the heart of Nike's success. The production of a training shoe is labour intensive so shifting manufacturing to countries in South East Asia which had low wage levels, compared to that of the USA, saves costs and increases profitability. Rather than setting up factories in SE Asia, Nike outsourced manufacturing completely to companies in the designated regions, thus reducing the need for capital investment in factories and equipment. ... this strategy has been criticised as abusing human rights of the workers in factories that offer poor pay and oppressive working conditions. But the company has turned this criticism to its advantage and made corporate responsibility a company priority. A potentially bad situation has been used as another opportunity for innovation and leadership.

(Source: OU Business School student assignment)

Text 1.10

Annotated version of Text 1.7

Essay text	Annotations
Explain why Nike is the biggest training shoe company in the world.	
For a company to be regarded as the biggest in its business sector it has to be successful. Nike is certainly a story of success. From its humble origins in the early 1970s to 43% market share in the USA, the success of Nike has been built on two strategies: marketing and innovation. This essay will examine how the marketing strategy and the company mission 'to bring inspiration and innovation to every athlete in the world' (Nike website, 2005) has built the company into a leading brand throughout the world.	Links to key concept *biggest* in title. Links biggest with *success*. Gives evidence of success (*43% market share*). States central argument (*built on two strategies*). 1 _____ _____ States purpose of essay.

Nike was launched in the USA in 1972 by Philip Knight, a former university runner with strong business acumen and his university coach, Bill Bowerman. Whilst studying at university Knight's business skills were evident when he produced a paper citing the benefits of producing sports shoes in countries with cheaper labour than the USA (a policy now implemented by all major training shoe companies). The major points of the paper were reduction of manufacturing costs and the concept that the appeal of a shoe was not in where it was made or how it was manufactured, but in the way that it was marketed.

First sentence signals 'this is background information' (*Nike was launched*).

2 _____

_____

Gives example of Knight's business skills.

Introduces the idea of *not manufacturing but marketing* which links to first key concept (*marketing*) in paragraph 1.

For Nike to compete with other brands of training shoe it has developed a marketing strategy to make the Nike brand highly desirable. The technique of communicating an 'image' is paramount in promoting the symbolic status of the goods it is selling. The marketing of the Nike brand draws upon an emotional appeal for the product that indicates individual success, personal achievement and self-fulfilment. The use of the famous 'Just do it' advertising slogan epitomises this marketing technique by intimating, in a vague manner, that with Nike shoes on your feet, anything is possible. Nike's advertising campaigns seek to 'shift the selling point away from the product itself and into a world of their own making' (Vanderbilt, 1998).

First sentence links to key concept *biggest* (*competewith other brands* = biggest).

Concept of *marketing strategy* links back to previous two paragraphs and frames this paragraph.

3 _____

_____

Introduces the concept of *advertising* which will link forward to next paragraph.

Training shoe companies invest a great deal of money in advertising to promote their products and convey the concept of emotional appeal. In 1998 Nike spent £10 million on advertising trainers in the UK alone; this was over twice the amount spent by Reebok and five times that spent by Adidas (Sturges, 2005, p. 33). The advertising portrays sporting stars as heroes who are also stylish and fashionable, emitting a message that sport is fashion.

4 _____

_____

Details used as evidence to support idea in first sentence.

[Paragraph on sports stars omitted]

Another aspect of the Nike marketing strategy is to use the technique of exclusivity to bolster the appeal of the brand. Nike use a method called 'tiered selling' to promote the trainer and create exclusivity. [*Keep on Running* video]. By only releasing a limited number of trainers (i.e. 5000) at the launch of a new design and selling them at carefully selected venues, Nike creates an exclusive 'club' of owners for a period of time until the shoe goes to the market in greater volume. This creates hype at launch and a demand for the product.

Innovation is another tool in the Nike success story, innovation in both business and technological terms. As mentioned previously, the idea of Philip Knight to focus on marketing the trainer rather than manufacturing it is at the heart of Nike's success. The production of a training shoe is labour intensive so shifting manufacturing to countries in South East Asia which had low wage levels, compared to that of the USA, saves costs and increases profitability. Rather than setting up factories in SE Asia, Nike outsourced manufacturing completely to companies in the designated regions, thus reducing the need for capital investment in factories and equipment. This strategy has been criticised as abusing human rights of the workers in factories that offer poor pay and oppressive working conditions. But the company has turned this criticism to its advantage and made corporate responsibility a company priority. A potentially bad situation has been used as another opportunity for innovation and leadership (Nike, 2004, *Corporate Responsibility Report*).

Omitted paragraph develops the theme of the previous paragraph.

Repeated concept word in first sentence (*marketing strategy*) and linking words (*another aspect*) link back to previous paragraphs.

5 _____

Lower level details in paragraph explain key concept (*exclusivity*) in first sentence.

Last sentence refers to increased *demand for product* and links this paragraph to the title – *Why is Nike the biggest?*

First sentence introduces new key concept from introduction (*innovation*) and links it to the title concept, *success.*
Linking words (*As mentioned previously*) used to link back to previous paragraphs.

6_____

_____

and uses other relevant business terms to do so (*low wage levels, costs, profitability, capital investment*).

7 _____

_____

but makes sure counterargument does not weaken main argument that *Nike = success.*

Nike has also been innovative in its design and technology application. The average development of a trainer is 18 months and design is paramount for consumer appeal, as Tom Vanderbilt (1998) explained '… design is what makes the product exciting, new and innovative.' Nike has spent enormous amounts of money on research and development and designs of its products. Since 1995 Nike has tripled its design budget and employs over 300 designers (Sturges, 2005, p. 24). Design is crucial to the commercial success of a product, especially in the training shoe market where style and technology combined produce a winning combination. Nike has led the way with technological advances in the training shoe market with developments such as the use of pockets of pressurised gas and waffle sole designs.

So in conclusion, the innovative approach of Nike of reducing overheads by outsourcing manufacturing of the training shoes in countries where labour costs are low, combined with focus on design and marketing has secured Nike the position of biggest training shoe company in the world. Nike has designed its products to be both functional and fashionable to appeal to target markets outside of sport. Successful marketing has created a brand known around the world and the Nike 'Swoosh' logo is instantly recognisable. Sponsorship of carefully selected sporting stars and slick advertising campaigns has promoted the Nike brand effectively. Nike has understood the environment in which to produce quality, affordable products and the market requirements to sell millions of shoes.

Repeats concept of *innovation* to link back to previous paragraph and link forward to this paragraph.

8 _____

_____

Gives details of investment in product innovations as basis for the idea that Nike is *innovative* in first sentence.

9 _____

_____

Winning combination links back to *success* in introduction.

Conclusion opens with signal words (*So in conclusion*) and the first sentence summarises the essay and links back to title (*biggest training shoe company in the world*).

10 _____

_____

The whole conclusion is a high level of generalisation.

Essay ends with a final high-level generalisation that reinforces the argument and repeats the key concepts of *innovation* and *marketing*.

Session 2

Text 2.1

Nike case study

[Paragraph 1]

Training shoes provide a good example of how making and selling a popular product works, what affects it, and what it itself influences.

[Paragraph 2]

In the UK, over £1 billion worth of training shoes were purchased in 1998. In 1997, Americans bought nearly 350 million pairs of training shoes – that is roughly one and a half pairs per head of the US population. Training shoes are a global product, that is, the same shoes are bought around the world. Global sales were worth $17 billion in 1998.

[Paragraph 3]

Just three companies dominate sales of training shoes worldwide: US-based Nike, and Reebok, US-owned, and Adidas, which is German-owned. Of the three, Nike is easily the biggest, especially in the USA, where it has a market share of 43%, compared with Reebok's 14% and Adidas's 12%.

[Paragraph 4]

Each of the leading trainer companies has a different heritage and culture. Nike, originally launched in the 1970s as a running shoe, has acquired the 'coolest' image, epitomised by its ubiquitous 'swoosh' logo and its memorable 'Just do it' catchline, now one of the best known advertising slogans in the world.

[Paragraph 5]

As one of the most powerful brand names in the world, Nike has also passed into economists' vocabulary. They refer to 'the Nike indicator', that is the supposed relationship between the company's business activities in Asian countries and the subsequent rise in those countries' standard of living.

[Paragraph 6]

The manufacture of training shoes is highly labour intensive. Leading companies like Nike and Adidas produce a large variety of shoe styles in relatively small numbers: new trainers are continually being introduced to reflect the latest tastes and trends, and old lines phased out. The rapid production changeovers this entails and the large number of parts comprising each trainer mean that there is no advantage to be gained from investing in dedicated machinery to manufacture a particular line. Compared with other products, therefore, trainers are still relatively 'hand made'.

[Paragraph 7]

Largely for this reason, by the mid-1980s most manufacturers had shifted production to countries such as South Korea and Taiwan, where labour costs were cheaper than in the USA. However, trainer companies went beyond simply transferring production abroad. They outsourced manufacturing completely to local firms in these countries, calculating that, since the shoe manufacturing process offered them little opportunity to gain competitive advantage over their rivals, they had no reason to invest in building expensive factories and purchasing manufacturing equipment. It is estimated that over 90 per cent of trainers sold are now manufactured in Southeast Asia.

[Paragraph 8]

In recent years, training shoe manufacturing has shifted from South Korea and Taiwan, now considered to be higher-cost production locations, to lower-cost ones such as Indonesia, Thailand and China. A small number of expatriate staff are employed by the trainer companies to oversee quality control.

[Paragraph 9]

Trainers are manufactured by assembly line production methods, using mainly female unskilled labour. Different stages of the production process do not necessarily take place in one location: the shoes may be made from components sourced in a range of countries other than the one in which they are finally assembled. For example, Nike's 'Air Max Penny', which is manufactured in South Korea and Indonesia, consists of 52 components made in five countries. It is estimated that each shoe is touched by 120 people during the manufacturing process.

[Paragraph 10]

Apart from a reduced wage bill, there are other advantages for training shoe businesses in making their shoes abroad and outsourcing production. Companies like Nike use a flexible network of overseas manufacturers, suppliers and distributors in order to produce their shoes 'just in time', that is, when the market needs them and in the exact quantities required. This means that they do not need to maintain other than minimum levels of stock, again saving costs.

[Paragraph 11]

They are also able to profit from beneficial trade and tariff agreements, wherever they exist, and from 'preferable' company legislation, which can make it easier to open and close factories at will.

[Paragraph 12]

In the early 1990s, the leading training shoe companies' strategy of using low-cost Asian labour to manufacture their products came under increasing scrutiny from human rights groups. By the end of the decade, campaign groups aimed at stamping out this so-called 'sweatshop' production were active in the USA, the UK and Australia.

[Paragraph 13]

Criticism has centred on three main aspects of manufacturing: who is employed; their conditions of employment; and the environment in which they work. It is no coincidence, it is argued, that the manufacture of training shoes takes place in countries such as Indonesia and China, which have repressive governments and weak labour unions. This, it is claimed, makes it easier for manufacturers to employ people management policies which would be unacceptable or even illegal in the West.

[Paragraph 14]

Independent research showed that many children were working in trainer factories, despite the existence of labour laws forbidding this. Employees were frequently paid very low wages, commonly below any minimum wage stipulated in the country where they worked. Working conditions were often poor, especially the air quality in factories; it was found that chemicals which were banned in the West were being used in the manufacture of trainers.

[Paragraph 15]

Initially, the trainer companies tried to divert criticism by claiming that the issue was the responsibility of their subcontractors, but were soon forced to respond when the subject was drawn to the attention of the US State Department. Eventually they were obliged to draw up codes of conduct in an attempt to eradicate human rights abuses in their factories, raise wages, ban harmful chemicals and eradicate the use of under-age labour. This was not sufficient for their critics; instead, it proved to be the first stage in a cycle of criticism and reaction which is still continuing, with the focus shifting from Indonesia to China and Vietnam, and manufacturers still struggling to establish a socially 'responsible' image.

[Paragraph 16]

While criticism of human rights abuses in training shoe factories is clearly justified, it is interesting to examine the trainer manufacturers' operations in the context of the prevailing economic situation in countries such as Vietnam and China. Their presence in these countries can be economically critical. China is now the biggest shoe producing country in the world; Nike is Vietnam's biggest employer. Jobs are scarce and people want to work for companies like Nike and Reebok. Factory jobs, while badly paid by Western standards, pay twice as much as teachers earn in Vietnam.

[Paragraph 17]

Nevertheless, as a result of the continued criticism, corporate responsibility is now a major concern for all trainer companies whose shoes are manufactured in Southeast Asia and China. For example, in 1998 Nike appointed its first new vice president for corporate and social responsibility and introduced six new corporate responsibility initiatives.

- Working conditions: The company guaranteed to ensure the changeover from use of solvent-based chemicals to use of water-based substitutes in its factories.

- Age limits: The minimum age limit for factory workers was raised to 18 in all footwear manufacturing. Footwear factory managers were obliged to guarantee not to employ anyone under this age.

- Independent monitoring: Nike pledged to secure independent monitoring of conditions in its factories by involving non-governmental organisations (aid agencies) in the process.

- Education: The company announced plans to expand in-factory education programmes in all Nike footwear factories.

- Small business finance: Support for a microfinance loan programme aimed at stimulating the establishment of small businesses in Vietnam, Indonesia, Pakistan and Thailand was increased.

- Research funding: Nike pledged to provide funding for research 'to explore issues related to global manufacturing and responsible business practices' such as independent monitoring and health issues.

[Paragraph 18]

The desire of training shoe companies to appear to be responsible corporate citizens extends beyond their practices in Southeast Asia to their activities in the USA and the UK, where they have shown themselves to be enthusiastic sponsors of 'worthwhile' community projects. Nike's concern for environmental issues is such that it has even sponsored the development of a process for recycling old training shoes in order to produce a substance from which sports pitches can be made. Nike has also responded to world crises such as Hurricane Mitch in Central America and the 1999 war in Kosovo by distributing footwear and clothing.

[Paragraph 19]

This demonstrates that, for trainer manufacturers, taking the issue of corporate responsibility seriously is not just a response to continued criticism, but is also perceived as an important means of establishing their credibility with their consumers, current and future, as they attempt to expand sales of their products throughout the world.

(Source: adapted from Sturges, J., 2000, 'Keep on running: the training shoe business', B200 *Understanding Business Behaviour*, Milton Keynes, Thanet Press Ltd/The Open University)

Text 2.2

Economic health

[Paragraph 1]

What is an economy?

An economy is a complex system for the exchange of resources between various stakeholders (also known as 'economic agents'). The two main economic agents in any economy are households and firms. They conduct the vast majority of exchanges. In most modern economies the exchanges that occur are made easier through the use of money, which also provides a means of measuring value within the economy. More recently, a third set of economic agents have developed, known as banks. In addition, at the national level, one of the great debates among economists is about the role of a fourth economic agent, the state government.

[Paragraph 2]

Now read Text 2.3 by Coates. This outlines a model of an economy and explores the relationships between these four economic agents. The model which is used to describe these relationships is called the 'circular flow of income'.

[Paragraph 3]

The relationship between businesses and the rest of the economy is two-way. While firms are reliant on the income provided from the various other economic agents, these other agents are also reliant on firms for their products and payments.

[Paragraph 4]

It is important to distinguish between two kinds of firms. Some firms (FIRMS 1) produce goods for household consumption (consumer goods), while other firms (FIRMS 2) produce materials and machines (capital goods) for use by FIRMS 1. The purchase of capital goods by FIRMS 1 is an example of investment. This is a key concept in understanding the economic environment.

[Paragraph 5]

The importance of investment

The reason investment is such an important concept is that most economists agree that high levels of investment are associated with a healthy economy. In other words, there appears to be a link between the level of investment and the general performance of the economy.

[Paragraph 6]

Let's start by considering what we mean by investment. Investment is that part of a firm's expenditure which increases or replenishes its stock of capital. Capital is anything purchased by the firm which is not immediately used up in the course of the firm's everyday operations, but retained and used to generate some future income. An example of this would be the cost of buying land and building new premises or that associated with the purchase of new equipment and any associated training for its use.

[Paragraph 7]

In all cases, businesses invest in order to generate a future reward or benefit for some or all of their stakeholders. For private-sector firms this may come in the form of increased profit or share value; whereas in the public and non-profit sectors it may come in the form of better or more cost-effective services to their clients or communities.

[Paragraph 8]

Investment is essential for the maintenance and development of any firm's business activities. However, it also has positive knock-on effects on other firms' incomes. These effects are multiplied as the income is passed on around the economic system. Take the example of a company's investment in a new fleet of trucks. The purchase of such equipment will pay the wages of those involved in their production – perhaps requiring additional labour to be employed to meet this demand. The initial injection of funds which this creates 'circulates' around the economy, generating income for a considerable number of people and businesses along the way. Overall, any increase in investment should therefore have a positive effect on the performance of the whole economy. Economists call this 'the multiplier effect'.

[Paragraph 9]

Measures of economic performance

At this point we must turn our attention to the performance of an economy. For most economists, understanding the relationship between investment and economic performance is one of the key objectives of their discipline. The four indicators outlined below are the most common measures of economic performance.

1   *Stability of employment*
    This is usually measured as the rate of unemployment or the proportion of available labour not bought and used by firms at a particular point in time.

2   *Living standards*
    This is usually measured as the rate of economic growth. This is the annual increase (or decrease) in Real Gross Domestic Product (Real GDP), that is to say, the total value of the products and services produced by the nation in a period, allowing for inflation.

3   *Price stability*
    This is usually measured as the rate of inflation. This is the rate at which the prices of products and services increase over a time period (usually a year).

4   *The balance of payments*
This is the net value of goods, services and resources exchanged between firms and households within the economy and foreign buyers and sellers.

[Paragraph 10]

One of the most noticeable aspects of these measures is their tendency to fluctuate if left unchecked, causing the confidence of firms and households to fluctuate as well. Consequently, governments tend to focus on a balance of these four in formulating and assessing the success of their economic policies.

[Paragraph 11]

Summary

A healthy economic environment is one which encourages all businesses to invest. Businesses which invest in capital projects are optimistic of future returns and at the same time are expressing their confidence in the economy they are investing in. By doing so they are also improving the economic environment for other businesses, through the 'multiplier effect'. All of this has a positive effect on economic growth and eventually on employment levels. For governments, a key policy aim is to help create an environment which stimulates and maintains that investment confidence.

[Paragraph 12]

In less developed economies, the firms with most power and influence are often very large multinational or global corporations. As a result, the economic environments in these countries become heavily reliant on inward investment from foreign firms. This certainly appears to benefit them in terms of economic growth but it can add to the air of instability within the economy.

(Source: adapted from Lucas, M., 2000, *Environments. Module 1 Study Guide*, Milton Keynes, The Open University Business School, pp. 22–30)

Text 2.3

Building a model of the economy

[Paragraph 1]

At its most elementary, it helps to think of the economy as a series of exchanges between two key economic institutions: between households (which among their other functions, provide labour power and consume products) and firms (who employ labour, and make products). The households supply workers to the firms and the firms supply goods and services to the households.

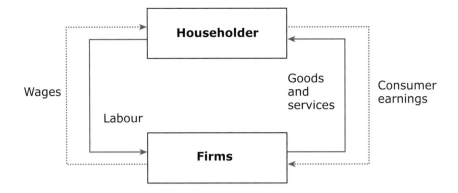

Figure 2.1   A model of the economy (Source: Coates, 2000, p. 56)

[Paragraph 2]

At the same time, spending flows round the circuit in the opposite direction. The firms pay the households' wages for the labour they supply, and the households pay the firms for the goods they obtain from them.

[Paragraph 3]

But life, of course, is not so simple. Banks and other financial institutions get into the act, as households deposit money with them, and as they lend money to firms, and to other households. The firms then use that money (and some of their income from the sale of goods and services to households) to buy machinery and raw materials from other firms – firms who don't themselves sell anything directly to households.

[Paragraph 4]

The government is in there as well, taxing some households and paying benefits to others, and taxing some firms and spending money to support others.

(Source: adapted from Coates, D., 2000, 'The management of the UK economy', in Lucas M. (ed.) *Understanding Business: Environments*, London, Routledge, pp. 55–7)

Text 2.4

A key concept-based outline

Explain why Nike is the biggest training shoe company in the world.

(A) Biggest?

- marketing and innovation

(B) History

- 1972 – Philip Knight and university coach, Bill Bowerman

- paper: producing sports shoes in countries with cheaper labour

(C) Marketing strategy

- Nike's advertising campaigns

- 'image'

- 'Just do it' advertising slogan

(D) Training shoe companies investment in advertising

- sporting stars as heroes

(E) Exclusivity

- 'tiered selling'

- exclusive 'club' of owners

(F) Innovation – business and technological

- Nike outsource manufacturing/South East Asia

- human rights in factories

- corporate responsibility

(G) Innovation – design and technology

- Tom Vanderbilt quote

- Nike tripled design budget since 1995

- technological advances in the training shoe market

- pockets of pressurised gas and waffle sole designs.

Conclusion

Text 2.5

A point-based outline

Explain why Nike is the biggest training shoe company in the world.

(A) Biggest?

= successful

humble origins to a 43% market share ← <u>marketing and innovation</u>

(B) History shows how founders had business skills

1972 – Philip Knight/Bill Bowerman

business skills: paper: producing sports shoes in countries with cheaper labour

→ reduction of manufacturing costs

& appeal ← how marketed.

(C) Marketing strategy

Nike's advertising campaigns → desirable brand

'image' → symbolic status of the goods

'Just do it' advertising slogan → individual success, personal achievement and self-fulfilment

(D) Training shoe companies advertising – high level of investment

sporting stars as heroes = sport is fashion

(E) Exclusivity – bolsters appeal of brand

'tiered selling' – promotes exclusivity

exclusive 'club' of owners – creates hype and demand

Conclusion

Extract 2.6

Explain why Nike is the biggest training shoe company in the world.

[...]

Innovation is another tool in the Nike success story, innovation in both business and technological terms. As mentioned previously, the idea of Philip Knight to focus on marketing the trainer rather than manufacturing it is at the heart of Nike's success. The production of a training shoe is labour intensive so shifting manufacturing to countries in South East Asia which had low wage levels, compared to that of the USA, saves costs and increases profitability. Rather than setting up factories in SE Asia, Nike outsourced manufacturing completely to companies in the designated regions, thus reducing the need for capital investment in factories and equipment. ... this strategy has been criticised as abusing human rights of the workers in factories that offer poor pay and oppressive working conditions. But the company has turned this criticism to its advantage and made corporate responsibility a company priority. A potentially bad situation has been used as another opportunity for innovation and leadership (Nike, 2004, *Corporate Responsibility Report*).

Nike has also been innovative in its design and technology application. The average development of a trainer is 18 months and design is paramount for consumer appeal, as Tom Vanderbilt (1998, p. 66) explained '... design is what makes the product exciting, new and innovative.' Nike has spent enormous amounts of money on research and development and designs of its products. Since 1995 Nike has tripled its design budget and employs over 300 designers (Sturges, 2005, p. 24). Design is crucial to the commercial success of a product, especially in the training shoe market where style and technology combined produce a winning combination. Nike has led the way with technological advances in the training shoe market with developments such as the use of pockets of pressurised gas and waffle sole designs.

So in conclusion, the innovative approach of Nike of reducing overheads by outsourcing manufacturing of the training shoes in countries where labour costs are low, combined with focus on design and marketing has secured Nike the position of biggest training shoe company in the world. Nike has designed its products to be both functional and fashionable to appeal to target markets outside of sport. Successful marketing has created a brand known around the world and the Nike 'Swoosh' logo is instantly recognisable. Sponsorship of carefully selected sporting stars and slick advertising campaigns has promoted the Nike brand effectively. Nike has understood the environment in which to produce quality, affordable products and the market requirements to sell millions of shoes.

(Source: OU Business School student assignment)

Session 3 resources

Text 3.1

Assignment title

Discuss the extent to which a large corporation such as Nike might influence the economic health of a developing country.

[Paragraph 1]

Wherever a large corporation such as Nike operates, the scale of its activity will have an effect on the locality. In a developing country, this activity might have a significant influence on the whole economy of the area. Economic commentators refer to 'the Nike indicator', assuming a clear link 'between the company's business activities in Asian countries and the subsequent rise in those countries' standards of living' (Sturges, 2000, p. 12). This essay will look at how much, and in which way, the business activities of a large corporation might influence the health of the economy in a developing country. It begins with an explanation of the terms 'economy' and 'investment' and then goes on to consider four indicators of economic health. Although multinational corporations' investment in developing countries is beneficial for such countries, there are some negative impacts as well.

[Paragraph 2]

An economy is 'a system for the exchange of resources ... between the various stakeholders within the economy' (Lucas, 2000, p. 22). In the model which has developed in the West, and which large corporations would operate throughout the world, the main economic agents are households, who supply labour and consume goods, and firms, who supply goods and 'consume' labour (Coates, 2000, p. 56). If work is created for a large number of people, this will have a significant impact on the exchange of resources. Nike is Vietnam's biggest employer (Sturges, 2000, p. 30). The influence this might have on the overall health of the economy can be assessed by a number of factors.

[Paragraph 3]

An important factor in economic well-being is investment. '... most economists agree ... that high levels of investment are associated with a healthy economy' (Lucas, 2000, p. 24). Nike does not invest directly in the developing countries where it operates, but it encourages others to invest by subcontracting the production of its shoes. Factories will be built and people will be employed, injecting money into the economy which will pass around and create more economic possibilities because of the 'multiplier effect'. An initial income will pass from hand to hand, consuming goods and creating new income with each transaction. This creates new demand for goods, which creates more demand for labour, and employs more people (Coates, 2000, p. 60). From the point of view of investment, a large corporation such as Nike has a very beneficial influence on the economic health of the developing countries in which it operates.

[Paragraph 4]

The wider picture of economic health is, however, more complicated. There are four indicators commonly used to measure economic performance: stability of employment, living standards, price stability, and balance of payments (Coates, 2000, p. 58). It is interesting to look at the influence of large corporations in each of these areas.

[Paragraph 5]

Stability of employment is not really a factor that companies like Nike are offering directly to the developing economies in which they operate. When costs increased in South Korea and Taiwan, for example, training shoe manufacturing was moved to lower cost locations such as Indonesia, Thailand and China (Sturges, 2000, p. 27). The benefit to the economies of Taiwan and Korea was not entirely lost, however, because 'the trend has been to continue to use the same Korean and Taiwanese manufacturers, who have set up and managed production plants in the new geographic locations' (Sturges, 2000, p. 27). The money brought into the economy by these firms should create employment indirectly. Therefore, although Nike does not offer stability of employment levels directly, its use of local companies as subcontractors is helping to create profits, which, if reinvested, can help employment levels.

[Paragraph 6]

The second economic indicator, rising living standards, requires an increasing flow of goods to consumers (Coates, 2000, p. 58). The money invested as a result of Western involvement should encourage the production of more goods, but until the infrastructure has time to develop, any increase in demand will cause prices to rise. The ability to control inflation and keep prices stable is the third indicator of economic health. In the short term, the influence of companies like Nike will make this difficult for a developing economy to achieve.

[Paragraph 7]

If local businesses do not develop to produce more goods to meet increased demand, there will also be a trend for consumers to buy goods produced elsewhere – imported goods. If a country is importing goods without exporting any goods, this will affect the balance of payments, which is the fourth indicator of economic health. Developing countries tend to be at a disadvantage in this area, as they lack both the financial expertise and the necessary capital to compete with the West.

[Paragraph 8]

The investment of large corporations such as Nike has an enormous influence on the economies of the countries where they operate. Money invested in an economy will multiply, and demand for goods will increase. In a developing economy, however, this will not necessarily help to create stable employment, rising living standards, price stability, or a favourable balance of payments – the indicators of a healthy economy.

[Paragraph 9]

It is encouraging that such companies have now become involved with initiatives to help achieve this, but it is unfortunate that the developing countries lose some of their unique identity as they strive to compete on Western terms. In the long term, the economic health of a developing country might be better served by a different vision of globalisation. 'Now is the time to realise that diverse values can partake of one economy. We need the background image of a choir of nations so that the peoples of the world can see their differences as "comparative advantages", enabling each to serve humanity in its own way' (Budd, 2006, p. 3).

References

Budd, C. H. (2006) 'Signs of the Times', in *Associative Economics Monthly*, January 2006, p. 3.

Coates, D. (2000) 'The management of the UK economy', in Lucas, M. (ed.) *Understanding Business: Environments*, Routledge, London, pp. 55–70.

Lucas, M. (2000) *Environments. Module 1 Study Guide*, The Open University Business School, Walton Hall.

Sturges, J. (2000) 'Keep on running: the training shoe business'. Case Study. *Understanding Business Behaviour*, Milton Keynes, The Open University Business School.

(Source: adapted from OU Business School student assignment)

Text 3.2

Discuss the extent to which a large corporation such as Nike might influence the economic health of a developing country.

[Paragraph 1]

In order to have a healthy economy it is important that the government maintains a balance between the management of demand, whether this is by consumers or investors, and the management of supply of money by investors and of goods by companies. As we are part of a global economy, factors such as imports and changes in the global economy impact on decisions in our own economy.

[...]

[Paragraph 2]

'Most economists agree ... that high levels of investment are associated with a healthy economy' ('Keep on running', p. 24). The introduction of one or more aspects of a business into a developing country brings with it money from the firm, skills to run the business operation, which could then filter through into the local community, and associated technologies. All of these factors have the potential to greatly influence a developing country's economy.

[Paragraph 3]

To examine how investment might influence the economy we can first look at the 'circular flow of income' model (Coates, 2000, pp. 56–8). There are four economic agents involved in this model: households, firms, banks and the government. Once income has been generated by a household, for example through its residents receiving payment by an employer, this money can be used to purchase goods and to pay taxes and therefore benefit the economy. The demand by households for goods and services from firms generates interest in this area, encouraging the businesses to invest in improving their services or increase the standard or choice of goods they have to offer. In order to invest in this way they are able to take out bank loans or sometimes receive government grants. This increases the flow of income and helps the economy to grow. Extra revenue can also be generated through the export of goods to other countries. This shows how investment by a company like Nike could help cash flow to circulate through a country's economy by offering jobs and wages to the residents.

[Paragraph 4]

Another example of how investment quickly accumulates and filters through an economy can be shown by the 'multiplier effect' (Coates, 2000, p. 60). This is where one sum of money can be distributed through society by an initial person investing a part of their total funds in a company, which retains some of what they have obtained and invests the rest in another person, product or service. The process then continues until the money is exhausted. If Nike were to give jobs to the community of a developing country the 'multiplier effect' could be implemented on a grand scale, the level of which would be determined by how many jobs were created and how much the workers received as payment.

[Paragraph 5]

Income is not the sole factor that helps to boost an economy however. Another tool that could do this is that of new and transferable skills and technology which would be introduced to the new Nike employees. Once a developing country, lacking in these skills, obtains this new knowledge it is possible that it could utilise it in other areas of society. This could help other businesses to flourish as they learn new skills. This is evident as Nike have set up factories in less developed countries such as South Korea and Taiwan and, along with making trainers for Nike, 'shoes for different companies are often manufactured simultaneously on neighbouring production lines' ('Keep on running', p. 26). It is possible that workers from these factories could one day leave and start up their own factories with these new skills and technological procedures, thus encouraging more economic growth.

[Paragraph 6]

I have so far discussed how a business like Nike could influence the economic health of a developing country, but it is possible that its influence on such an economy could be minimal, due to the phenomenon of globalisation. Thanks to 'deregulation, technological advances and financial management innovations' (Rastogi, 2000, p. 75), even poorer countries are able to sustain a stable economy by trading with other, richer countries. Deregulation has led to 'the opening of the world economies (which) has resulted in more international trade and increased capital among countries' (Rastogi, 2000, p. 78) and this international trade results in capital being brought into these countries and so investment from Nike would not necessarily be required as much as in previous times. Therefore, the influence on the economy may be minimal.

[Paragraph 7]

To conclude, a large company such as Nike could greatly influence the economic health of a developing country through investing in new business operations there, thus bringing new jobs to the communities involved. Investment is crucial to a healthy economy and funds are dispersed through society via the multiplier effect and the circular flow of income. Investment need not only be in the form of currency, it can also be introduced as new skills and technology which will benefit the running of the country if they are then used in areas of the country other than that which they were first introduced. By using these forms of investment a company like Nike could influence the economic health of a developing country, but how much the economy was influenced would depend on how much investment was made as well as how much global trade is already influencing the country's economy.

References and bibliography

Coates, D. (2000) 'Identifying environmental issues', in Lucas, M. (ed.) *Understanding Business: Environments*, London, Routledge, , pp. 55–70.

Lucas, M. (2000) *Environments. Module 1 Study Guide*, Milton Keynes, The Open University Business School.

The Open University Business School (2000) 'Keep on running: the training shoe business'. Video, VC1188. *Understanding Business Behaviour*, Milton Keynes, The Open University Business School.

Rastogi, D. (2000) 'Living without borders', in Lucas, M. (ed.) *Understanding Business: Environments*, London, Routledge, pp. 75–8.

Sturges, J. (2000) 'Keep on running: the training shoe business'. Case Study. *Understanding Business Behaviour*, Milton Keynes, The Open University Business School.

(Source: adapted from OU Business School student assignment)

Session 4 resources

Text 4.1

The role of the market

Markets bring together buyers and sellers of goods and services. In some cases, such as a local fruit stall, buyers and sellers meet physically. In other cases, such as the stock market, business can be transacted over the telephone or internet, almost by remote control. We need not go into these details. Instead, we use a general definition of markets.

A *market* is a shorthand expression for the process by which households' decisions about consumption of alternative goods, firms' decisions about what and how to produce, and workers' decisions about how much and for whom to work are all reconciled by adjustment of *prices*.

Prices of goods and of resources, such as labour, machinery and land, adjust to ensure that scarce resources are used to produce those goods and services that society demands.

Much of economics is devoted to the study of how markets and prices enable society to solve the problems of what, how, and for whom to produce. Suppose you buy a hamburger for your lunch. What does this have to do with markets and prices? You choose the café because it was fast, convenient and cheap. Given your desire to eat, and your limited resources, the low hamburger price told you this was a good way to satisfy your appetite. You probably prefer steak but that is more expensive. The price of steak is high enough to ensure that society answers the 'for whom' question about lunchtime steaks in favour of someone else.

[...]

There were several markets involved in your purchase of a hamburger. You and the café owner were part of the market for lunches. The student working behind the counter was part of the local labour market. The café owner was part of the local wholesale meat market and the local market for rented buildings. These descriptions of markets are not very precise .... That is why we have adopted a very general definition of markets which emphasises that they are arrangements through which prices influence the allocation of scarce resources.

(Source: adapted from Yates, C. St J., 1992, *Economics*, Englewood Cliffs, NJ, Prentice Hall, pp. 20–21)

Text 4.2

Types of market failure

In the real world, markets frequently fail to achieve social efficiency. Part of the problem is the existence of 'externalities', part is a lack of competition, and part is the fact that markets may take a long time to adjust to any disequilibrium, given the often considerable short-run immobility of factors of production.

Externalities

The market will not lead to social efficiency if the actions of producers or consumers affect people *other than themselves*. These effects on other people are known as externalities: they are the side-effects, or 'third-party' effects, of production or consumption. Externalities can be either desirable or undesirable. Whenever other people are affected beneficially, there are said to be external benefits. Whenever other people are affected adversely, there are said to be external costs.

Thus the full costs to society (the social costs) of production of any good or service are the private costs faced by firms plus any externalities of production. Likewise the full benefits to society (the social benefits) from the consumption of any good are the private benefits enjoyed by consumers plus any externalities of consumption.

There are four major types of externality.

External costs of production (MSC > MC)

When a chemical firm dumps waste in a river or pollutes the air, the community bears cost additional to those borne by the firm. The marginal social cost (MSC) of chemical production exceeds the marginal private cost (MC).

[...]

The problem of external costs arises in a free-market economy because no one has legal ownership of the air or rivers and can therefore prevent or charge for their use as a dump for waste. Control must, therefore, be left to the government or local authorities.

Other examples of external costs of production include extensive farming that destroys hedgerows and wildlife, acid rain caused by smoke from coal-fired power stations, and nuclear waste from nuclear power stations.

External benefits of production (MSC < MC)

Imagine a bus company that spends money training its bus drivers. Each year some drivers leave to work for coach and haulage companies. These companies' costs are reduced as they do not have to train such drivers. Society has benefited from their training (including the bus drivers themselves, who have acquired marketable skills), even though the bus company has not. The marginal social cost of the bus service, therefore, is less than the marginal private cost.

[...]

Another example of external benefits in production is that of research and development. If other firms have access to the results of the research, then clearly the benefits extend beyond the firm which finances it. Given that the firm only receives the private benefits, it will conduct a less than optimal amount of research. Similarly, a forestry company planting new woodlands will have a beneficial effect on the atmosphere.

External costs of consumption (MSB < MB)

When people use their cars, other people suffer from their exhaust, the added congestion, the noise, etc. These 'negative externalities' make the marginal social benefit [MSB] of using cars less than the marginal private benefit [MB] (i.e. marginal utility to the car user).

[...]

Other examples include noisy radios in public places, cigarettes and their smoke, and litter.

External benefits of consumption (MSB > MB)

When people travel by train rather than by car, other people benefit by there being less congestion and exhaust and fewer accidents on the roads. Thus the marginal social benefit of rail travel is greater than the marginal private benefit (i.e. the marginal utility to the rail passenger). There are external benefits from rail travel.

Other examples include deodorants, vaccinations, and attractive clothing.

In general, whenever there are external benefits, there will be too little produced or consumed. Whenever there are external costs, there will be too much produced or consumed. The market will not equate MSB and MSC.

(Source: adapted from Sloman, J. and Sutcliffe, M., 1998, 'When markets fail', in Suneja, V. (ed.), 2000, *Understanding Business: Markets*, London, Routledge, pp. 148–9)

Text 4.3

Firms and social responsibility

It is often assumed that firms are simply concerned to maximize profits: that they are not concerned with broader issues of social responsibility. What this assumption means is that firms are only concerned with the interests of shareholders (or managers) and are not concerned for the well-being of the community at large. It is then argued, however, that competitive forces could result in society benefiting from the self-interested behaviour of firms: i.e. that profit maximization will lead to social efficiency under conditions of perfect competition and the absence of externalities. But, as we have seen, in the real world markets are not perfect and there are often considerable externalities. In such cases, a lack of social responsibility on the part of firms can have profoundly adverse effects on society. Indeed, many forms of market failure can be attributed directly to business practices that could not be classified as 'socially responsible': advertising campaigns that seek to misinform or in some way deceive the consumer; monopoly producers exploiting their monopoly position through charging excessively high prices; the conscious decision to ignore water and air pollution limits, knowing that the chances of being caught are slim.

(Source: adapted from Sloman, J. and Sutcliffe, M., 1998, 'When markets fail', in Suneja, V. (ed.), 2000, *Understanding Business: Markets*, London, Routledge, p. 159)

Text 4.4

Ignorance and uncertainty

Perfect competition assumes that consumers, firms and factor suppliers have perfect knowledge of costs and benefits. In the real world there is often a great deal of ignorance and uncertainty. Thus people are unable to equate marginal benefit with marginal cost.

Consumers purchase many goods only once or a few times in a lifetime. Cars, washing machines, televisions and other consumer durables fall into this category. Consumers may not be aware of the quality of such goods until they have purchased them, by which time it is too late. Advertising may contribute to people's ignorance by misleading them as to the benefits of a good.

Firms are often ignorant of market opportunities, prices, costs, the productivity of factors (especially white-collar workers), the activity of rivals, etc.

Many economic decisions are based on expected future conditions. Since the future can never be known for certain, many decisions will be taken that in retrospect will be seen to have been wrong.

(Source: adapted from Sloman, J. and Sutcliffe, M., 1998, 'When markets fail', in Suneja, V. (ed.), 2000, *Understanding Business: Markets*, London, Routledge, p. 150)

Text 4.5

Ignorance and uncertainty

[S1] Lack of information and uncertainty can also lead to market failure. [S2] Perfect competition assumes that consumers, firms and factor suppliers have perfect knowledge of costs and benefits – often this is not the case. [S3] Consumers may only purchase some products or services once and therefore have no previous experience on which to base their decision, exacerbated by advertising messages and persuasive sales techniques. [S4] Similarly, firms are often ignorant of market opportunities, prices, costs, rival activity, productivity of factors, etc. [S5] Consumer and organisational decisions made in the absence of sufficient information can often be wrong and result in market failure.

(Source: OU Business School student assignment)

Text 4.6

Public goods

There is a category of goods that the free market, whether perfect or imperfect, will underproduce or may not produce at all. They are called public goods. Examples include lighthouses, pavements, flood control dams, public drainage, public services such as the police and even government itself.

Public goods have two important characteristics

If I walk along a pavement or enjoy the benefits of street lighting, it does not prevent you or anyone else doing the same. There is thus what we call non-rivalry in the consumption of such goods. These goods tend to have large external benefits relative to private benefits. This makes them socially desirable, but privately unprofitable. No one person on their own would pay to have a pavement built along his or her street. The private benefit would be too small relative to the cost. And yet the social benefit to all the other people using the pavement may far outweigh the cost.

If I spend money erecting a flood control dam to protect my house, my neighbours will also be protected by the dam. I cannot prevent them enjoying the benefits of my expenditure. This feature of non-excludability means that they would get the benefits free, and would therefore have no incentive to pay themselves. This is known as the free-rider problem.

When goods have these two features, the free market will simply not provide them. Thus these public goods can only be provided by the government or by the government subsidising private firms. (Note that not all goods and services produced by the public sector come into the category of public goods and services: thus education and health are publicly provided, but they can be, and indeed are, privately provided.)

(Source: adapted from Sloman, J. and Sutcliffe, M., 1998, 'When markets fail', in Suneja, M. (ed.), 2000, *Understanding Business: Markets*, London, Routledge, pp. 150–1)

Extract 4.7

Mario's text

There are a lot of socially desirable public goods, including pavements, street lights, police, government, national health care and schools because MSB exceeds MPB. The good thing about them is that anyone can freely enjoy the benefits of these without having to pay for the costs. Because non-excludability, non-rivalry and free-rider issues make such goods privately unaffordable, there's a bit of a problem, though – the free market would never provide them.

(Source: adapted from OU Business School student assignment)

Extract 4.8

Marina's text

Another area of market failure is in the provision of public goods. These are goods 'that the free market, whether perfect or imperfect, will underproduce or may not produce at all' (Sloman and Sutcliffe, 1998, p. 150). Public goods include items such as pavements, public drainage and public services such as defence and education. The reason markets fail to provide public goods is that they are usually non-rival and non-excludable goods. Non-rival goods are those where everyone benefits from their use but individuals would rarely pay to purchase the product unilaterally. Non-excludable goods, such as national defence, are those where it is impossible to stop others benefiting from the product and thus it is difficult to get them to pay for the product. In both of these instances the goods are 'socially desirable, but privately unprofitable' (Sloman and Sutcliffe, 1998, p. 150) and so the market fails to deliver a socially desirable outcome. In the matter of public goods it is usually left to the government to provide the service through taxation or subsidising the markets to provide them.

(Source: OU Business School student assignment)

Extract 4.9

Peter's text

Another source of market failure is the market mechanism's inability to produce vital public goods. Public goods are items for which you can't charge according to consumption. No-one can enjoy their benefits exclusively; others are not prevented from doing the same (known as non-rivalry and non-excludability of consumption). Examples of public goods include: national defence, police, street lighting and pavements. As you can enjoy the goods for free there is no incentive to pay for them and similarly no incentive for organisations to produce them, as they will not be paid by consumers to do so. Consequently, these goods have to be financed by Government (with compulsory taxation revenues) (Sloman and Sutcliffe, 1998, p. 151). The Government bureaucracy involved can be complex and costly. Direct provision or overseeing of public services can also be difficult as the Government's ability to prioritise and provide these goods efficiently can be affected by electoral considerations and private and state employee interests, particularly within developing countries. In an extreme example, high levels of corruption within the Kenyan Government have involved ministers and civil servants paying as much state cash as possible for shoddy goods or services never rendered, in relation to the transport system (The Economist, Jan 2006).

(Source: OU Business School student assignment)

Extract 4.10

Alan's introduction

Critically discuss why markets may fail to deliver socially desirable outcomes.

The market in its simplest form is a system of voluntary arrangements between firms, which consume labour and supply goods, and households, which supply labour and consume goods. Supporters of a free market economy suggest that if allowed to operate without interference the market will deliver outcomes that make the best use of resources to the benefit of all. There are several reasons why this may fail to happen.

(Source: OU Business School student assignment)

Extract 4.11

Barbara's introduction

Critically discuss why markets may fail to deliver socially desirable outcomes.

The market, from a liberal view, is 'the site of the exchange of goods and services by free agents pursuing their own aims' (Brown, 1991, p. 135). This assumes perfect competition, and Brown explains how this market should therefore provide socially desirable outcomes:

> Self-interested behaviour best promotes the wealth of nations through the free and undisturbed play of market forces. Here the market is seen as an efficient co-ordinator of the activities of

free individuals, where the interplay of demand and supply in a competitive market is the 'key to prosperity' for everyone. (1991, p. 118)

'Prosperity', however, is not always reality. Sloman and Sutcliffe (1998, p. 147) explaining that the two main socially desirable outcomes of the market are social efficiency and equity, show how a liberal free market fails to deliver these. This is summarised by Wall (2002, p. 151):

the allocation of resources is for some reason inefficient and could therefore be improved to make at least some people better off. Markets fail to provide public goods; markets fail when there is some degree of monopoly power; markets fail when costs of production do not reflect the true costs to society.

This paper explores and expands on these causes of market failure. It concludes that all are present in free markets because the 'self-interest' denies the market to operate in society's best interest.

(Source: OU Business School student assignment)

Extract 4.12

Marina's introduction

Critically discuss why markets may fail to deliver socially desirable outcomes.

In order to discuss why markets fail to deliver socially desirable outcomes, we need to consider what is understood by market failure. Having defined the criteria for market failure it will be necessary to discuss the factors that can contribute to this failure and how this can create socially undesirable outcomes. How markets can create inequity in wealth and income distribution and potential government reactions to these circumstances must also be considered. It will be necessary to give pertinent examples of market failure to aid this discussion.

(Source: OU Business School student assignment)

Extract 4.13

Mario's conclusion

Critically discuss why markets may fail to deliver socially desirable outcomes.

In conclusion, markets fail to deliver socially desirable outcomes as they fail to internalise external costs and benefits of production and consumption. Although government interventions could rectify the issue of externalities to some extent, some risks of government failure would be involved. It is more ideal if firms take social responsibilities with their own incentives while governments provide minimum levels of support to maintain the consistency of regulations and protection of life, freedom and rights.

(Source: OU Business School student assignment)

Extract 4.14

Peter's conclusion

Critically discuss why markets may fail to deliver socially desirable outcomes.

In summary, the market is limited in its ability to deliver socially desirable outcomes. Various factors lead to social inefficiencies and market failure, namely: externalities, public goods, inappropriate consumer preferences in relation to merit goods, lack of information to make rational choices, the effect of monopolies and oligopolies and the immobility of factors of production. There are a variety of additional factors that lead to socially inequitable outcomes: unequal initial distribution of resources, unequal access to career advancing opportunities and unequal bargaining power. Possible remedies to market failure in terms of Government intervention include: taxation and subsidy payments to combat externalities; direct provision of public goods, legislation and authorities to prevent long term monopolies, provision of accurate statistical information to the market place; consumer information and awareness programmes; taxation and welfare provisions to redistribute incomes. Private organisations can also play their part along with Government intervention. They can self-regulate and set their own targets related to energy efficiency and ensure social responsibility towards all stakeholders and not just shareholders. It is this combination of market and non market mechanisms that should be utilised to achieve socially desirable outcomes.

(Source: OU Business School student assignment)

Text 4.15

Critically discuss why markets may fail to deliver socially desirable outcomes.

line 1   In order to discuss why markets fail to deliver socially desirable outcomes we need to consider what is understood by market failure. Having defined the criteria for market failure it will be necessary to discuss the factors that can contribute to this failure and how this can
5   create socially undesirable outcomes. How markets can create inequity in wealth and income distribution and potential government

reactions to these circumstances must also be considered. It will be necessary to give pertinent examples of market failure to aid this discussion.

10   When discussing market failure we are not looking at a Stock Market crash or the inability of a supermarket to provide enough turkey near Christmas. Markets are considered to have failed when they do not produce enough of a product to optimise public consumption or when they produce a product that, despite its consumption, may have
15   detrimental effects on society. They are also considered to have failed when their actions deliver an unfair imbalance in income, wealth, power and other economic resources. This can be simplified as 'markets may fail to generate socially efficient outcomes and may fail to deliver equitable outcomes' (Suneja, 2000, p. 145).

20   Some of the factors that cause markets to fail are called externalities. Externalities are factors that do not directly affect the cost of production or the cost of consumption of a product but will produce an indirect cost that society will have to pay. There are externalities that produce benefits that markets also fail to deliver. Externalities can
25   generally be broken down into 4 areas. The external costs of production are those that do not affect the price of production but cause other problems or costs. An obvious example is pollution. Production by-products that pollute the air or water near factories do not add to the cost of production but incur a cost to the community.
30   'The problems of external costs arise in a free-market economy because no one has legal ownership of the air or rivers and can therefore prevent or charge for their use as a dump.' (Sloman/ Sutcliffe, 1998, p. 148). The Chernobyl nuclear plant explosion could be viewed as an extreme example of an external cost of production. In
35   such instances the market has failed because it has ignored the marginal social cost of the pollution or considers it to be someone else's problem.

External costs of consumption are the negative effects on society caused by the consumption of products, but which the consumer is not
40   charged for. Examples of these are such things as car exhaust fumes and cigarette smoke. Again the market has failed due to the disregard of the side effects of the product. In cases like this the products are often overproduced and heavily advertised with little or no mention of the hazards involved with consumption.

45   There are externalities that produce benefits for example training or education. For example a company hires a group of workers and then trains them but later some of these workers move to another company. The individuals, the new company and society have all benefited from the initial training, but have not paid for it. This is
50   considered to be an external benefit of production. In instances like this markets fail due to the fact that they will limit the amount spent on externalities like training that may benefit their competitors. This is a failure to maximise the potential of its workforce and therefore socially undesirable.

55   Healthcare is an area where there are obvious externalities of consumption. If people had access to unlimited cheap, or free, medical care; were given access to vaccination for common ailments or were

aided in living healthier lives then society would benefit in numerous ways. However, in markets where there are obvious external benefits

60   of consumption, invariably the market fails to produce sufficient of the product to deliver a socially desirable outcome.

When looking at the externalities involved in market failure it is possible to simplify the matter by saying 'whenever there are external benefits, there will be too little produced or consumed.

65   Whenever there are external costs, there will be too much produced or consumed.' (Sloman/Sutcliffe, 1998, p. 149). The market fails to deliver socially desired outcomes in instances where externalities are involved because in a capitalist market the marginal cost or benefits to society are ignored in favour of profit for the market. This is also

70   an example of the use of power and inequity. Companies generate increased profits and wealth for themselves, their executives and shareholders at the expense of the consumer and society who foot the bill. Another area of market failure is in the provision of public goods. These are goods 'that the free market, whether perfect or imperfect,

75   will underproduce or may not produce at all.' (Sloman/Sutcliffe, 1998, p. 150). Public goods include items such as pavements, public drainage and public services such as defence and education.

The reason markets fail to provide public goods is that they are usually non-rival and non-excludable goods. Non-rival goods are

80   those where everyone benefits from their use but individuals would rarely pay to purchase the product unilaterally. Non-excludable goods, such as national defence, are those where it is impossible to stop others benefiting from the product and thus it is difficult to get them to pay for the product. In both of these instances the goods are

85   'socially desirable, but privately unprofitable' (Sloman/Sutcliffe, 1998, p. 150) and so the market fails to deliver a socially desirable outcome. In the matter of public goods it is usually left to the government to provide the service through taxation or subsidising the markets to provide them.

90   Having looked at some of the reasons why markets fail to deliver socially desirable outcomes it is possible to say that these failures are not imposed on markets but the market chooses to fail in certain areas. It can be said that markets exercise their power over which areas it will succeed in and which areas it will fail in. The use of

95   market power is in line with the market model proposed by Professor Amartya Sen. In capitalist markets, where profit often dominates policy; large companies can use their economic power to operate in the most profitable markets or in the most profitable manner. They can also use their economic power to generate an unequal

100   distribution of wealth and economic resources, which may be seen as a failure of capitalist markets in general. Failure to produce public goods, unless appropriately subsidised by government, is a use of economic power. Overproduction in markets with external costs, usually to increase profits, and underproduction in market with

105   external benefits, so as to not benefit those who do not pay for a product, are both examples of the use of economic power. Invariably external costs and lack of external benefits are most keenly felt by those at the lower end of the economic power spectrum or with less disposable income. In looking at things this way we can agree with

110   the idea 'Sen is saying that the balancing is of power and muscles, and in such a contest the weak must inevitably come off worst.' (Brown, 1991, p. 137).

Having defined what we understand by the term market failure, it is patently obvious that markets fail to deliver socially desirable
115   outcomes in a variety of ways. Externalities of production and consumption will usually mean that markets overproduce products with an external social cost or underproduce products with an external social benefit and therefore fail to deliver socially desirable outcomes. However, underlying the obvious signs of market failure
120   may be the fact markets opt to exercise their power in a capitalist system and therefore choose to fail in certain areas. Failure to deliver socially desirable outcomes may often increase profits or force the government to pay the market to produce an otherwise unprofitable product. In both of these instances society may see this as a failure
125   but the markets may not.

(Source: OU Business School student assignment)

Session 5 resources

Text 5.1

Multinational corporations – an introduction

[Paragraph 1]

[Earlier] we looked at one of the important dimensions of international economic activity, namely international trade. There are also other ways by which economic agents can participate in international economic activity: an important example of this is the operation of multinational corporations (MNCs).

[Paragraph 2]

MNCs are firms that own or control productive assets in more than one country. It is this ownership or control of foreign assets that distinguishes multinationals from firms that do business overseas by simply exporting goods or services. There is a great deal of diversity in the nature of the world's multinationals, in terms of their size, the nature of their business, ownership pattern and organisational structure. The big MNCs are very big indeed: the largest 200 control more than one-third of total world production, and many have a turnover that exceeds the GDP of whole nations.

[Paragraph 3]

Firms may decide to go multinational for a variety of reasons. Sometimes the chief motivation is the reduction in costs, such as labour costs, costs of raw materials and components, and transport costs. At other times, the growth motive is more important: a firm may wish to exploit any advantages that it has over its rivals (such as the ownership of superior technology or managerial expertise) in foreign markets. By going multinational, a firm may also be able to spread its fixed costs and hence exploit economies of scale.* These economies of scale may be related to production, marketing, procurement or research and development (R&D). The desire to circumvent import restrictions may be another motivation for firms to become multinational. Firms can 'jump' tariff barriers by locating their operations behind tariff walls. What other reasons are there for firms going multinational?

[Paragraph 4]

When a firm goes multinational, it may face various problems in the process of doing so. These include problems relating to operating in a new and unfamiliar environment, and co-ordination of the activity of subsidiaries located in different parts of the world. Cross-cultural issues can be particularly hard to manage. If multinationals become too big and do not manage their international operations very well, they may then suffer from diseconomies of scale.

* Economies of scale = reduction in cost of production due to a large number of items being produced.

(Source: adapted from Suneja, V., 2000, B200 *Markets Module 2 Study Guide*, Milton Keynes, The Open University)

Text 5.2

Multinational corporations

Since the mid-1980s multinational businesses have been downsizing. They have been shrinking the size of their headquarters, removing layers of bureaucracy, and reorganising their global operations into smaller autonomous profit centres. Gone is the philosophy that big companies will inevitably do better than small ones. In fact, it now appears that multinationals are seeking to create a hybrid form of business organisation, which combines the advantages of size (i.e. economies of scale) with the responsiveness and market knowledge of smaller firms.

The key for the modern multinational is flexibility, and to be at one and the same time both global and local.

[Here] we shall consider why it is that businesses decide to go multinational, and evaluate what impact they have on their host countries. Before we do this we shall first offer a definition of multinational business and assess the importance of multinational investment for the UK economy.

What is a multinational corporation?

There are some 35 000 multinational corporations[1] (MNCs) worldwide. Between them they control a total of 15 000 foreign subsidiaries. Furthermore, the top 200 MNCs control about one-third of global production.

Even given their obvious gigantic size and overwhelming importance within the global economy, MNCs defy simple definition. At the most basic level, an MNC is a business that either owns or controls foreign subsidiaries in more than one country.

It is this ownership or control of productive assets in other countries which makes the MNC distinct from an enterprise that does business overseas by simply exporting goods or services. However, merely to define an MNC as a company with overseas subsidiaries fails to reflect the immense diversity of multinationals.

Diversity among MNCs

Size
Many, if not most, of the world's largest firms – IBM, Shell, General Motors, etc. – are multinationals. Indeed, the turnover of some of them exceeds the national income of many smaller countries (see Table 5.1).

And yet there are also thousands of very small, often specialist multinationals, which are a mere fraction of the size of the giants.

Table 5.1 Comparison of the ten largest multinational corporations and selected countries according to size of annual GDP, 1990

MNC rank	Country or company (headquarters)	1990 GDP or gross sales (US$bn)
1	General Motors (USA)	125.1
	Indonesia	107.3
2	Royal Dutch/Shell (UK/Netherlands)	107.2
3	Exxon (USA)	105.9
	Norway	105.8
4	Ford Motors (USA)	98.3
	Turkey	96.5
	Argentina	93.2
	Thailand	80.1
5	IBM (USA)	69.0
6	Toyota (Japan)	64.5
7	IRI (Italy)	61.4
8	British Petroleum (UK)	59.5
9	Mobil (USA)	58.8
10	General Electric (USA)	58.4
	Portugal	56.8
	Venezuela	48.3
	Philippines	43.8
	Malaysia	42.4
	Colombia	41.1
	Nigeria	34.7
	Egypt	33.2
	Bangladesh	22.8
	Kenya	7.5

(Source: M.P. Todaro, *Economic Development*, 6th edn (Longman, 1997), p. 536.)

The nature of business
MNCs cover the entire spectrum of business activity, from manufacturing to extraction, agricultural production, chemicals, processing, service provision and finance. There is no 'typical' line of activity of a multinational.

Overseas business relative to total business
MNCs differ in respect to how extensive their overseas operations are relative to their total business. Nearly 50 per cent of IBM's sales and profits come from its activities outside the USA. The foreign operations of other MNCs represent only a small fraction of their total business.

Production locations
Some MNCs are truly 'global', with production located in a wide variety of countries and regions. Other MNCs, by contrast, only locate in one other region, or in a very narrow range of countries.

There are, however, a number of potentially constraining factors on the location of multinational businesses. For example, businesses concerned with the extraction of raw materials will locate as nature dictates! Businesses that provide services will tend to locate in the rich markets of developed regions of the world economy, where the demand for services is high. Others locate according to the factor intensity of the stage of production. Thus a labour-intensive stage might be located in a developing country where wage rates are relatively low, while another stage which requires a high level of automation might be located in an industrially advanced country.

Ownership patterns

As businesses expand overseas, they are faced with a number of options. They can decide to go it alone and create wholly owned subsidiaries. Alternatively, they might share ownership, and hence some of the risk, by establishing joint ventures. In such cases the MNC might have a majority or minority stake in the overseas enterprise.

In certain countries, where MNC investment is regulated, many governments insist on owning or controlling a share in the new enterprise. Whether governments insist on domestic companies (or themselves) having a majority or minority stake varies from country to country. It also depends on the nature of the business and its perceived national importance. For example, until recently the Indian government insisted on having a majority stake in all multinational business ventures in the high-technology sector of the Indian economy.

Organisation structure

[Elsewhere we have] discussed the variety of organisational forms that MNCs might adopt – from the model where the headquarters, or parent company, is dominant and the overseas subsidiary subservient, to that where international subsidiaries operate as self-standing organisations, bound together only in so far as they strive towards a set of global objectives.

The above characteristics of MNCs reveal that they represent a wide and very diverse group of enterprises. Beyond sharing the common link of having production activities in more than one country, MNCs differ widely in the nature and forms of their overseas business, and in the relationship between the parent and its subsidiaries.

Multinational corporations and the UK economy

When looking at the role played by MNCs in the UK economy, we need to distinguish between UK companies operating overseas, and foreign companies operating in the UK.

We can estimate the size of multinational investment, by both UK business and overseas companies, by looking at figures for foreign direct investment (FDI). FDI represents the finance used either to purchase the assets for setting up a new subsidiary (or expanding an existing one), or to acquire an existing business operation.

Figure 5.1(a) that between 1985 and 1989 outward direct investment rose by £12.1 billion (a rise of nearly 140 per cent). In 1990, however, it fell to half its 1989 level. Since 1991 outward direct investment has risen steeply again, standing at £28.6 billion in 1996, the largest ever recorded figure for direct investment overseas.

Inward direct investment into the UK increased steadily from 1985 to 1989, reaching £18.6 billion. In 1991 inward investment fell to £9.1 billion and for the following three years showed no signs of recovery, falling to £6.1 billion in 1994. Between 1994 and 1996, however, overseas direct investment into the UK increased by £14.7 billion to £20.8 billion. As with outward investment, the 1996 figure for inward direct investment is the highest ever recorded (see Figure 5.1b).

(a)

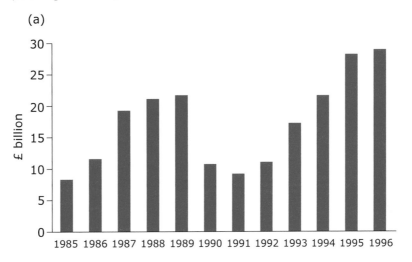

(b)

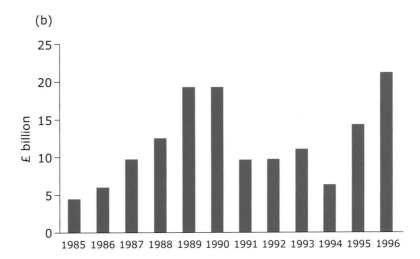

Figure 5.1 Direct investment into and out of the UK, 1985–96: (a) direct investment overseas by UK residents; (b) direct investment in the UK by overseas residents (Source: *Financial Statistics* (ONS))

The income earned from direct foreign investment is shown in Figure 5.2: both that received from UK investment overseas (credits) and that paid to overseas investors in the UK (debits). The figure shows that since 1985 the UK has experienced a steadily rising surplus of direct investment income. In 1985 the surplus stood at a modest £0.2 billion. By 1995 the surplus had risen to £12.9 billion. In other words, direct investment income credits have risen significantly faster than debits. This is particularly so since 1993.

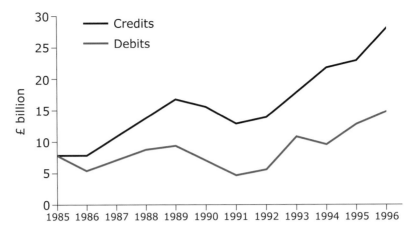

Figure 5.2 Direct investment income, 1985–96 (Source: *UK Balance of Payments: the Pink Book* (ONS))

FDI and the UK economy: international comparisons

By international comparisons, the UK is both a major investor overseas and a significant receiver of foreign direct investment. During the late 1980s, the USA was the largest receiver of UK direct investment, receiving approximately 70 per cent of all direct investment funds. However, in recent years the USA's share has fallen, and the European market has received greater attention from UK business. Given the moves towards establishing a single European market, such a trend is hardly surprising.

After Canada, the UK is the largest recipient of inward direct investment, receiving approximately 10 per cent of the world's total. In 1995 the UK's stock of inward direct investment stood at £150 billion, over three times the level recorded ten years earlier.

In respect to the European market, which attracts two-fifths of all US, Japanese and South Korean investment, latest figures suggest that approximately 40 per cent of all manufacturing inward investment into the European Union comes to the UK.

Before we consider the potential costs and benefits resulting from having a large multinational sector within the economy, we will first investigate what businesses can hope to gain from going multinational.

Why do businesses go multinational?

There are many reasons why companies choose to go multinational. These will depend on the nature of their business and on their corporate strategy. Before identifying the various motives for producing overseas rather than merely exporting to such countries, it is necessary to distinguish different categories of multinational.

Categories of multinational

A horizontally integrated multinational[1]. This type of multinational seeks to produce essentially the same product in different countries (but perhaps with some variations in product specification to suit the needs of the local market). The primary objective of this strategy is to achieve growth by expanding into new markets.

---

[1] A multinational that produces the same product in many different countries.

A vertically integrated multinational[2]. In this case, the multinational undertakes the various stages of production in different countries for a core business. Thus in some countries it will go backwards into the business's supply chain to the components or raw materials stages, and in others it will go forwards into the product's assembly or distribution. Oil companies such as Shell and Exxon (Esso) are good examples of vertically integrated multinationals, undertaking in a global operation the extraction of crude oil, controlling its transportation, refining it and producing by-products, and controlling the retail sale of petrol and other oil products. The principal motive behind such a growth strategy is to be able to exert greater control over costs and reduce the uncertainty of the business environment.

A conglomerate multinational[3]. Such multinationals will produce a range of different products in different countries. By this process of diversification, conglomerate multinationals will look to spread risks, and maximise returns through the careful buying of overseas assets. The Hanson Corporation is a good example of a conglomerate multinational, having overseas interests ranging from diamond extraction in the Republic of South Africa, to owning the global fast-food chain Burger King.

We can see from the above classification that a clear distinction can be made between MNCs that are using their multinational base primarily as a means of reducing costs [...] and those that are using it to achieve growth [...] Let us now consider how, by going multinational, such goals might be achieved.

Reductions in costs

Nations, like individuals, are not equally endowed with factors of production. Some nations are rich in labour, some in capital, some in raw materials. In other words, individual nations might have specific advantages over others. Because such factors of production are largely immobile, especially between nations, businesses respond by becoming multinational: that is, they locate where the necessary factors of production they require can be found. In the case of a business that wishes to extract raw materials, it has little choice but to do this. But why might a business wish to move for labour? Here it is not simply a question of the availability of labour: rather it is a question of the relative cost of labour. For example, it might locate an assembly plant in a developing country (i.e. a country with relatively low labour costs), if that plant uses large amounts of labour relative to the value added to the product at that stage. Thus foreign countries, with different cost conditions, are able to provide business with a more competitive environment within which to produce its products.

Cost differences between countries are ruthlessly exploited by Nike, the American sportswear manufacturer. Nike has organised itself globally such that it can respond rapidly to changing cost conditions in its international subsidiaries. Its product development operations

---

[2] A multinational that undertakes the various stages of production for a given product in different countries.

[3] A multinational that produces different products in different countries.

are carried out in the USA, but all of its production operations are subcontracted out to over 40 overseas locations, mostly in south and south-east Asia. If wage rates, and hence costs, rise in one host country, then production is simply transferred to a more profitable subsidiary. So long as Nike headquarters has adequate information regarding the cost conditions of its subsidiaries, management decision making concerning the location of production simply follows the operation of market forces.

The location of multinational operations does not simply depend on factor prices: it also depends on factor quality. For example, a country might have a highly skilled or highly industrious workforce, and it is this, rather than simple wage rates, that attracts multinational investment. The issue here is still largely one of costs. Highly skilled workers might cost more to employ per hour, but if their productivity is higher, they might well cost less to employ per unit of output. It is also the case, however, that highly skilled workers might produce a better quality product, and thus increase the firm's sales.

If a country has both lower-priced factors and high-quality factors, it will be very attractive to multinational investors. In recent years, the UK government has sought to attract multinational investment through its lower labour costs and more flexible employment conditions than those of its European rivals, while still having a relatively highly trained labour force compared with those in developing countries.

Locating production in a foreign country can also reduce costs in other ways. For example, a business locating production overseas would be able to reduce transport costs if those overseas plants served local or regional markets, or used local raw materials. One of the biggest cost advantages concerns the avoidance of tariffs (customs duties). If a country imposes tariffs on imports, then, by locating within that country (i.e. behind the 'tariff wall'), the MNC gains a competitive advantage over its rivals which are attempting to import their products from outside the country, and which are thus having to pay the tariff.

Costs might also be reduced as a consequence of the host government's attitude towards MNC investment. In an attempt to attract inward investment, a government might offer the MNC a whole range of financial and cost-reducing incentives, many of which help reduce the fixed (or 'sunk') costs of the investment, thereby reducing the investment's risk. The granting of favourable tax differentials and depreciation allowances, and the provision of premises are all widely used government strategies to attract foreign business. A recent case in the UK saw a potential investor offered financial incentives valued at £37 000 per employee to locate production in an area of Wales!

In highly competitive global markets, even small cost savings might mean the difference between success and failure. Thus MNCs will be constantly searching for ways of minimising costs and locating production where the greatest advantage might be gained.

Growth strategy

Once markets within the domestic economy have become saturated, and opportunities for growth diminish, dynamic firms may seek new markets and hence new opportunities by expanding production overseas. [...] [B]usinesses can look to expand in one of two ways: through either internal or external expansion. MNCs are no exception to this rule. They can expand overseas, either by creating a new production facility from scratch (such as Nissan in the north-east of England), or by merging with or taking over existing foreign producers (such as the acquisition of Rover by BMW).

Expanding by becoming multinational enables the business to spread its risks (it is no longer tied to the trade cycle of any one country or region, or to the specific market conditions of one particular country), and in addition it enables the business to exploit any specific advantages it might have over its foreign rivals in their home markets. Such advantages might include the following.

- **The ownership of superior technology.** Given the dominant market positions that many MNCs hold, their possession of the most up-to-date technology is to be expected, and likely to be one of the principal keys to their success. Such ownership will not only enhance the productivity levels of the MNC, but probably also contribute to the production of superior-quality products.

- **Entrepreneurial and managerial skills.** With the arrival of Japanese multinationals in the UK, it became instantly apparent that Japanese managers conducted business in a very different way from their British counterparts. The most fundamental difference concerned working practices. Japanese MNCs quickly established themselves as among the most efficient and productive businesses in the UK ....

- **Research and development capacity.** Like big business generally, MNCs are likely to invest heavily in R&D in an attempt to maintain their global competitiveness. The global scale of their operations allows them to spread the costs of this R&D over a large output (i.e. the R&D has a low average fixed cost). MNCs, therefore, are often world leaders in process innovation and product development.

[...]

The product life cycle and the multinational company

One way in which the MNC might exploit its dominant position – in particular, its R&D advantage – is by extending the life cycle of a given product. By shifting production overseas at a particular point in the product's life cycle, the business is able to reduce costs and maintain competitiveness. In the domestic market, it might be faced with growing competition and static (or even declining) demand. Rivals might also be busy copying its technology. By extending (or switching) its production to different geographical locations, where demand is still growing, where there is less competition and where it has a technological advantage over any local companies, its profitability can be more effectively maintained in the long run.

The product life cycle hypothesis [has been] discussed at length [elsewhere]. However, it is worth reviewing its elements here in order to identify how an MNC, by altering the geographical production of a good, might extend its profitability.

A product's life cycle can be split into four phases: launch, growth, maturity and decline.

The launch phase
This will tend to see the new product produced in the economy where the product is developed. It will be exported to the rest of the world. At this stage of the product's life cycle, the novelty of the product and the monopoly position of the producer enable the business to charge high prices and make high profits.

The growth phase
As the market begins to grow, other producers will seek to copy or imitate the new product. Prices begin to fall. In order to maintain competitiveness, the business will look to reduce costs, and at this stage might consider shifting production overseas to lower-cost production centres.

Maturity
At the early stage of maturity, the business is still looking to sell its product in the markets of the developed economies. Thus it may still be happy to locate some of its plants in such economies. As the original market becomes increasingly saturated, however, the MNC will seek to expand into markets overseas which are at an earlier stage of development. Part of this expansion will be by the MNC simply exporting to these economies, but increasingly it will involve relocating its production there too.

Maturity and decline
By the time the original markets are fully mature and moving into decline, the only way to extend the product's life is to cut costs and sell the product in the markets of developing countries. The location of production may shift once again, this time to even lower-cost countries. By this stage, the country in which the product was developed will almost certainly be a net importer (if there is a market left for the product), but it may well be importing the product from a subsidiary of the same company that produced it within that country in the first place!

Thus we can see that the ability to transfer production to different locations reduces costs and enables profits to be made from a product that could have become unprofitable if its production had continued from its original production base.

Problems facing multinationals

In the vast majority of cases, businesses go multinational for sound business and economic reasons, which we have outlined above. However, multinational corporations may face a number of problems resulting from their geographical expansion:

Language barriers. The problem of language is less of a difficulty in the developed economies of the world than it is in the developing markets of, for example, Africa or Latin America. The more that the MNC employs expatriate rather than local staff, the greater the problem will be.

Selling and marketing in foreign markets. Strategies that work at home might fail overseas, given wide social and cultural differences. Many US multinationals, such as McDonald's and Coca-Cola, are frequently accused of imposing American values in the design and promotion of their products, irrespective of the country and its culture. This can lead to resentment and hostility in the host country, which may ultimately backfire on the MNC.

Attitudes of host governments. Governments will often try to get the best possible deal for their country from multinationals. This could result in governments insisting on part ownership in the subsidiary (either by themselves or by domestic firms), or tight rules and regulations governing the MNC's behaviour, or harsh tax regimes. In response, the MNC can always threaten to locate elsewhere.

Communication and co-ordination between subsidiaries. Diseconomies of scale may result from an expanding global business. Lines of communication become longer and more complex. These problems are likely to be greater, the greater is the attempted level of control exerted by the parent company: in other words, the more the parent company attempts to conduct business as though the subsidiaries were regional branches. Multinational organisational structures where international subsidiaries operate largely independently of the parent state will tend to minimise such problems.

(Source: adapted from Sloman, J. and Sutcliffe, M., 1998, in Suneja, V. (ed.), 2000, *Understanding Business: Markets*, London, Routledge, pp. 196–204)

Text 5.3

Asda Wal-Mart case study

Whether it's the environment, product sourcing, healthcare, wages, community involvement or diversity, we are investing in the future. We have an aggressive vision. With courage and commitment to change, we will be at our best and remain true to the legacy of the company Sam Walton founded some 43 years ago.

Lee Scott, Wal-Mart CEO, 25 October 2005

Asda is currently operationally failing.

Andy Bond, Asda Wal-Mart CEO, 13 December 2005

When the *Fortune* list of the top five hundred companies was published in 1955, Wal-Mart did not even exist. It began with one self-service store in the geographically isolated south-western corner of the United States in 1962. By 2003 its 1386 supercenters (based on the European 'hypermarket' model) had captured 19% of the US grocery market and 16% of pharmacy sales (with management aspirations to reach 35% and 25% respectively over the next five years).

Looking beyond the United States, with 5000 stores and wholesale clubs across ten countries, by 2002 Wal-Mart was No. 1 in the Fortune list of the top 500 companies. It was the largest retail chain, the largest company and the biggest employer in the world (standing at 1.6 million employees – or 'associates' in Wal-Mart's preferred terminology – in 2005). The worth of Wal-Mart's trade with China outstrips that of the UK and, if it were a country, it would match the economies of Sweden and Austria. In both 2003 and 2004 it was Fortune's 'Most Admired Company', accounting for 2% of US GDP.

[...]

The Wal-Mart approach

So how had the business founded by Sam Walton in Bentonville, Arkansas in 1962 assumed a position of global domination a mere 40 years later? Had it all been plain sailing? And what can we learn from the Wal-Mart experience?

The entrepreneur, Sam Walton, was an innovator right from the start. He pioneered the concept of self-service and central billing (rather than paying separately for goods purchased in different departments as had been the norm in the past). Wal-Mart was about 'Everyday low prices' (EDLP) and one-stop family shopping. There were three 'core values':

- Respect for the individual
- Service to our customers
- Strive for excellence.

Through to the 1980s the company's expansion was built on this approach in its home territory – small rural towns with little or no competition. Outside the immediate area Wal-Mart had a low profile but Walton built a substantial chain of stores right across the south-western states and then moved beyond, to take on the competition. Although the company was often hailed as a job creator and regenerator by local chambers of commerce, other commentators began to suggest that the Wal-Mart strategy was based on moving into an area, driving smaller competitors out of business by undercutting on prices and then consolidating its own outlets into larger and fewer outlets, thereby undermining local economies and, in the longer term, making consumers travel further for their shopping.

It was however, from the company's point of view, a successful expansion strategy. By 1990 it was the largest retailer in the United States and in 1991 moved into Mexico, with Canada following in 1994 – becoming the largest in both of those two countries as well. Throughout the decade its global growth intensified, mainly using a combination of buy-outs and joint ventures.

The Asda takeover

In the UK it was the supermarket chain Asda that 'joined the Wal-Mart family' when it was taken over on 26 July 1999.

Asda itself had been founded in 1965 by a group of Yorkshire farmers. (The name came from the merger of the Asquith chain of three supermarkets and Associated Dairies.) It expanded into the south of England in the seventies and eighties but found itself overstretched in 1989 when it acquired the superstores belonging to rival chain, Gateway; it was also trying to sell too broad a product range and in 1991 and again in 1993 it had to ask shareholders for money to stave off insolvency. During this troubled period in the early 1990s its fortunes were restored under the leadership of Archie Norman, recruited as CEO from the Kingfisher Group in 1991. He moved on to become Chairman from 1996 to 1999 when he entered politics as a front bench Conservative MP. As CEO, Norman took Asda back to its roots as a food retailer, concentrating on building market share on the back of low prices rather than the loyalty schemes being developed by its major competitors at that time.

When Wal-Mart acquired the Asda chain it had 229 stores. Following the take-over several 'Asda-Wal-Mart Supercentres' were opened, based on the US model, with the Wal-Mart name appearing in the UK with the first such supercentre in Bristol. By mid 2004 there were 259 stores and 19 depots, mostly in Scotland or northern England, employing some 122,000 'colleagues'.

> I have long been an admirer and I went on a pilgrimage to Wal-Mart's headquarters in 1994. [...] I came away thinking that they had something we had got to have. In many ways I think this is coming home."
>
> Archie Norman, Asda-Wal-Mart former CEO, 1999

There was always going to be a good fit between Asda and Wal-Mart, with Asda's marketing already reflecting the focus on low prices (EDLP) that had been at the very heart of Wal-Mart's US marketing strategy. In 2001 Asda slashed prices by some £52million, introducing a range of over 400 'smart price' food products based on Wal-Mart's budget brand. The 'Asda Price' campaign and the smiling face 'rollback' campaign, borrowed from Wal-Mart, set out to position Asda as the most affordable supermarket in the UK, a claim that did not go unchallenged by its competitors. In August 2005 the Advertising Standards Agency (ASA) upheld a complaint by rivals Tesco that Asda's claims were based on limited and unrepresentative surveys which excluded low cost supermarkets such as Aldi and Lidl altogether. The ASA found that Asda's information did indeed lack transparency and did not truly reflect its position relative to the whole UK market.

In the first five years after acquisition, Asda's grocery market share increased from 13 to 16% without acquiring any new stores and by 2005 Asda was the second biggest supermarket chain in the UK, although with market share in the mid-teens, a long way behind Tesco which approached 30%. In its larger stores Asda has followed the Wal-Mart strategy of increasing sales space by removing backroom areas and increasing non-food sales areas, including its 'George' line of clothing. This increase in non-food sales areas left other supermarkets struggling to catch up. Sales growth in non-food lines rose by 25% and the ability to source jointly with Wal-Mart meant that these new lines were offered at prices not before matched in the UK market – toasters, kettles and irons for under £8.00 for example. In the US around 30% of Wal-Mart's total sales come from its 'Speciality Division'. This includes a diverse range of products such as car rental, holidays, hotel discounts and optical, photographic and pharmacy services. In the UK, Asda has begun to expand into these areas too. In 2005 it added one million square feet of retail space and announced the intention of a similar growth target in 2006.

In common with other supermarkets, Asda has changed its strategy in relation to out of town/edge of town retail developments, a change forced on the industry by government regulations and planning controls to curb further hypermarket developments. The battle for new store sites came back firmly onto the High Street and towards the end of 2005 Asda also announced plans to open a range of small 'community' discount stores, selling almost entirely Asda own-label products but under a different name.

For some time there was speculation that Asda was the favourite to take over the Safeway chain of supermarkets in the UK, although that prize eventually went to competitors, Morrisons. During the bidding period, however, there was real concern voiced in some quarters that if Asda and Safeway had merged, they would have formed a retailing force that not even Tesco would have been able to compete with. Asda has, however, bought a number of former Safeway stores as part of the sale forced by the UK government's competition regulations and there have been persistent rumours that Asda Wal-Mart also has a predatory eye on the discount clothing retailer, Matalan.

Some problems

However, the Asda picture has not been entirely rosy. With food price deflation in the UK running at 1–2%, Asda's market share actually fell in 2005. While Asda's annual growth of 2% was running behind industry growth rates of 3%, Sainsbury's had been slowly regaining ground this year under chief executive Justin King with many industry commentators anticipating that it might lose its number two position to Sainsbury's in coming months. In a year where the business had twice failed to meet the targets set by Wal-Mart, there was clearly something which had gone amiss and Andy Bond, Asda CEO, expressed the view that the business had become 'drunk on its own success' and taken its eye off the ball in terms of new business opportunities.

So it appears that the Wal-Mart formula has not been an automatic key to success everywhere, including in the UK. Much has been made of the strength of the Wal-Mart culture in developing its US base but it has not always displayed a cultural sensitivity as it has sought to expand into other parts of the world.

The Wal-Mart cheer

Give me a W!
Give me an A!
Give me an L!
Give me a Squiggly!
Give me an M!
Give me an A!
Give me an R!
Give me a T!
What's that spell?
Wal-Mart!

Whose Wal-Mart is it?
My Wal-Mart!
Who's number one?
The customer! Always!

In Germany, staff expressed unhappiness with the expectation that they would join in the 'Wal-Mart morning cheer' (inspired by a visit Walton had once made to a shoe factory in Korea). Employee morale was badly hit by Wal-Mart's rules and regulations. Although they were operating in Germany, the official company language remained English and US managers made no attempt to learn German, leading to serious communication problems with German-speaking staff.

Likewise, the conservative customers did not all appreciate the attentions of the Wal-Mart 'Greeters', at the entrance to every store. If the company had failed to understand the local culture it had also underestimated the competition from existing market leaders and the 'Hard Discount' (HD) stores which were pioneered in Germany, with limited own-label product ranges, no racks and goods typically kept in cartons on the floor and prices around 30% lower than those of national brands. These pose tough competition for Wal-Mart.

The company also hit problems with German labour laws and other aspects of government legislation. Wal-Mart had bruising encounters with the well established German trade union movement. Union leaders sought to force the company to join an employers association and sign collective wage agreements. When they refused to do so, there was significant strike action among employees and damaging publicity. The German government also took legal action against the company for selling staples like sugar, milk and margarine below cost price – in contravention of legislation. Wal-Mart also found itself in breach of commercial regulation by refusing to publish profit and loss accounts and a balance sheet. The trade unions sued Wal-Mart in the German courts, who ordered that the information be put in the public domain and levied heavy fines on senior Wal-Mart managers in Germany.

In Argentina, Wal-Mart failed to appreciate local idiosyncrasies and in Japan, it was widely reported that its cookies were too sweet for local tastes. Yet, here and other places, the company may have made mistakes initially but has proved itself quick to embrace change and learn from those mistakes, engineering turnaround in both.

Cultural change and values

With the takeover of Asda in the UK, Wal-Mart's HR bosses recognised the challenge of introducing the 'Wal-Mart culture' while at the same time preserving staff loyalty and commitment. Systems change was certainly required to integrate the business and its operations but, beyond this, according to Wal-Mart Resourcing Manager, Philip Horn,

> The intention was to launch a tidal wave of change across the whole organisation – to find an innovative, intriguing and swift means of creating an organisation of productive, committed employees who love what they do.

Wal-Mart brought in a firm of consultants who offered a 'Gung Ho! Change process'. Starting with the Directors, followed by 800 mid to top-level managers, the training initiative was introduced by an announcement in the form of a card sent personally to each participant announcing that 'The world is full of surprises'. When it was opened it released a paper butterfly and a message from the CEO with the dates of the three-day training event. The training itself was held in a circus-style marquee decorated in a Native American theme, complete with forest, river, totem pole, beaver dam and flying geese. The company's mission statement and values were carved in rough stone and beanbag seating doubled as rocks. At night, participants slept in log cabins and cooked for one another.

Some commentators attribute the company's strategic success to its ability to get the small things right. Sam Walton was, by all accounts, a charismatic and powerful figure who led by example. The three beliefs, which underpinned the organisational values, he inculcated: respect, service and excellence, he turned into rules in terms of how he expected everyone in the business to behave. The 'Ten foot rule' decreed that any member of staff coming within ten feet of a customer should look them in the eye and ask if there was anything they could do to help. The 'Sundown rule' meant that any request coming in during the day should have a response by the close of business.

Rule 1 – the customer is always right

Rule 2 – if the customer is wrong, refer to Rule 1

It might be easy to dismiss this as a somewhat 'folksy' approach to marketing but that would be to seriously underestimate the operational excellence that came to underpin EDLP. Combining the company's sustained low pricing with good service, convenience and a stock control system, which meant that the goods were available on the shelves, has, many would suggest, been at the heart of the Wal-Mart success story.

Family businesses are often vulnerable when the founder stands down. Wal-Mart had always been a family business (with five of its family members still among the richest ten people in the world). Only one of Sam's sons, Rob Walton, had lengthy experience in the company and when Sam stood aside in the early 1990s Rob became Chairman – although Chairman rather than Chief Executive, which many observers took as evidence that Sam Walton's historical emphasis on the team rather than the individual was being translated into a succession plan which meant that, although family involvement would continue, it was the professional executive team led by the CEO which would maintain and build upon the values and beliefs that Walton had brought to the business so far. Although Sam Walton, as founder, has not been an element of the company's external marketing strategy, he has continued to be a powerful and iconic figure within internal marketing. In terms of executive succession planning too, the business has continued to both promote from within and to manage the succession of CEOs with an assurance that has seen such handovers barely register a blip on its stock market value.

In the immediate post-Walton era from 1995 onwards there were five cultural imperatives that drove both expansion and consistency across the divisions of the company:

- stock it
- price it right
- show the value
- take the money
- teach them.

The best way to make a sale was to ensure that the product was in stock, at the right price, that customers should be shown why they should buy it and that, in taking the money, cashiers should be friendly and hospitable. 'Teach them' refers to staff training and instructions.

Sources of success?

Wal-Mart had always been renowned for its frugality. It was not unusual for executives to be expected to share hotel rooms and Sam himself drove a 1984 pick-up truck. Part of this legacy was to continue in the approach to driving down costs, both internally and in relation to suppliers, but this should not be equated with risk adversity. Sam himself had borrowed millions of dollars to finance expansion in the early years. CEO David Glass was to put billions at stake in pioneering the development and implementation of IT and distribution systems that would provide the technological base to underpin the business's widely respected operational excellence.

In the 1960s Wal-Mart was out in front in introducing computers, in the 1970s the use of POS (point of sale) data. The 1980s brought electronic data exchange (EDS) and universal product codes (UPC) and the 1990s real-time tracking of goods right through the supply chain. In the early years of the 21st century Wal-Mart has been developing ground-breaking RFID programmes (Radio Frequency Identification Technologies) and 'cross-docking' to ensure that items remain warehoused for as short a time as possible. All of this had been essential to compensate for the lower profit margins that come with the EDLP philosophy. The company's reputation in the logistics field was such that when Amazon wanted to establish its warehousing and distribution systems, it was key Wal-Mart managers that it sought to hire.

When Wal-Mart took over Asda in the UK it bought a company that had already developed its own processes and systems but it quickly became clear that to benefit from the leverage afforded by being part of Wal-Mart, Asda would have to quickly move over to the standard Wal-Mart corporate systems. Starting with a high-level analysis and a change management process to get buy-in at all levels – from boardroom to accounts clerks – there was a meticulously planned and structured 18-month programme of activity and implementation – including managing the technical interface with suppliers. Over this period every single core financial system was replaced with no business disruption (and a parallel growth in sales to a ten-year high). As Ian Leighton, the then Asda CEO, said:

This is the biggest and most complex systems change programme in the history of British retail.

The company had built its global presence and capacity without putting in place regional structures or lengthy and complex communication and supply chains. This meant that Headquarters (or 'Home Office' in Sam's preferred parlance) could stock-take any item in any store in the world in less than an hour. Yet this IT capacity was not about remoteness. Traditionally top executives had spent four days a week in stores and managers were highly visible. (On finding one whose staff claimed that they saw little of him, Sam provided a prompt by locking his office door.)

This 'open door' policy was extended into the sharing of information with both 'associates' and suppliers with daily and weekly sales figures openly available, allowing adjustments in the supply chain and as a motivator for staff who have also been heavily engaged in providing local intelligence about opportunities to increase sales based, in part, on limited scope for local pricing taking competition into account. The company's powerful data-mining tools were used not only extensively internally but also externally to analyse local demographics and population profiling. The 'store of the community' program in the USA developed local stocking, particularly taking into account the ethnic diversity of different areas. An illustration of this introduced in Asda-Wal-Mart in 2005 was the sale of 'Ramadan' calendars with chocolate treats for children in areas with significant Muslim populations.

In Dortmund in Germany local managers found that their target population contained more than an average number of relatively young single people and introduced Friday evening 'singles' shopping nights (with red ribbons available to tie on trolleys and special 'flirting zones' in selected aisles.) The store claimed a 15% increase in sales, suggested that around 30 couples had met in this way and patented the idea so that competitors could not follow suit.

Wal-Mart may have been Fortune's 'Most admired' company two years running but the size, scale and business methods of the 'Beast of Bentonville' have not brought it universal adulation. Some have commented on the cult-like nature of its organisational culture and its staff have been referred to as 'Wal-Martians'. Its practices have come under scrutiny by trade unions: it has been firmly anti-union since its inception on the grounds that unionisation would drive up costs (and commentators estimate that it pays its associates 20–30% less than unionised competitors). The company has responded by offering profit-sharing and share-option schemes to all employees (rather than restricting them to senior executives which has more commonly been the case).

Wal-Mart has also been the subject of more legal action than any other company. In December 2005, Wal-Mart was ordered to pay US $172m (£99m) in compensation to workers in California who were refused lunch breaks. A California court found Wal-Mart broke a state law requiring employers to give staff an unpaid 30-minute lunch break if they worked more than six hours. More than 100,000 Wal-Mart employees in California will be eligible for compensation.

Wal-Mart stores are popular for their low prices, but critics accuse them of achieving success by denying workers' rights.

In the United States Wal-Mart employs significant numbers of women in low paid and part-time roles and has been the subject of a class action on gender discrimination. Consumer and community groups have challenged the conventional wisdom that Wal-Mart should be welcomed as a job-creator, citing evidence of a pattern whereby it uses its purchasing power and EDLP to drive under the competition. Between 1992 and 2003, commentators suggested that it drove some 13,000 traditional US supermarkets out of business. It has also created a pattern of opening smaller stores on the edge of towns which destroy local economies and then consolidating these smaller stores into 'supercenters' which mean that consumers have further to travel and there are corresponding reductions in job numbers because of economies of scale. Anti-globalisation campaigners have pointed to the company's increasing outsourcing of production to south-east Asia and it has come under sustained pressure to provide the evidence to support its much vaunted ethical stance in relation to both wage rates and the employment of child labour.

In the UK, after a long period of being hailed as a model employer, Asda has increasingly come under fire from charity and trade union sources for planning a 'strategic assault' on its staff working conditions, with the aim of cost reduction and increased productivity. According to documents leaked to the GMB Trade Union, the company would like to introduce 'single man loading' for jobs that involve lifting, even where risk assessment underlines the need to have two people working on such tasks. They would also like to encourage supervisors to 'lead by example' in taking shorter breaks and rest periods and to remove the right of staff to have access to the arbitration service ACAS.

War on Want has claimed that Wal-Mart keeps its prices low across the world by strict working regimes in its supermarkets and depots as well as demanding ever-reducing prices from its suppliers, including those in the developing world. Wal-Mart has countered these claims by referring to independent audits of all its factories and its compliance with ethical trading initiatives. Its low prices, the company say, are built on its high volumes and economies of scale.

Towards the end of 2005, Wal-Mart was again in expansionist mode, acquiring the Brazilian operations of Portuguese retailer Sonae for US$757 million and announcing a major expansion of supercenters in Canada. Some US retail analysts have pointed to the general slowing in US sales growth and suggested that it is only through expanding into different countries that Wal-Mart would be able to meet its bold and aggressive growth targets. Against this backdrop, its stock market value was stagnant in 2004 and down 5% up to December 2005. While its international operations only account for some 20% of its overall sales, the eventual target is a third. At the end of 2005, it was operating in 15 countries outside the USA but commentators point to its patchy track record, with its struggles in Japan, patchy performance in Germany and, more recently, the acknowledged troubles at Asda in the UK. Mexico, however, is thriving.

While Brazil is a large market, it already has clear and well established market leaders and there are already brutal price wars raging in parts of Canada. According to recent analysis by Merrill Lynch, Wal-Mart has had substantially lower returns on its international operations (6%) as distinct from its US performance (24%). Even so, they would see international operations as positive, given their contribution to revenue and earnings growth overall.

In 2004, Lee Scott, Wal-Mart CEO, was voted by *Vanity Fair* magazine as the world's most powerful person, ahead of both Bill Gates and Rupert Murdoch.

(Source: adapted from case study for B200 TMA 07, 2005)

Session 6 resources

Text 6.1

[Paragraph 1]

MNCs may potentially bring a lot of benefits to the host nation. They may raise the growth rate of the host nation by bringing in new investment, new technologies or managerial competencies. They may stimulate inter-firm competition and thereby induce their domestic rivals to become more innovative and competitive. MNCs may also promote the development of various supporting industries or complementary industries.

[Paragraph 2]

MNCs may, however, also bring in several costs for the host economy. Sometimes MNCs may enjoy such a huge competitive advantage over local firms that they can destroy local competition rather than promoting it. At other times, they may not promote the development of any local economic activity but simply source their components from abroad. They may repatriate most of their profits rather than reinvesting it in the domestic economy. MNCs may also pose serious regulatory problems for host governments because of their 'footloose' nature. Their ability to relocate their activities internationally may also increase uncertainty and insecurity for a nation's work force. Multinationals may also be able to avoid paying their due share of taxes to national governments by practising transfer pricing.

[Paragraph 3]

The issue of costs and benefits of multinational activity is particularly important in the context of developing countries. Developing countries may potentially gain from certain kinds of foreign direct investment that bring in appropriate technology, managerial know-how and finance. Foreign direct investment may help in closing a developing country's savings gap and its foreign exchange gap. On the other hand, foreign direct investment in developing countries may have many undesirable consequences. It may distort the development priorities and goals of a developing country away from poverty reduction and provision of basic needs, and towards maximising the growth in national income. Multinationals may through their advertising power be able to create demands for products that only a few can afford. The technology that they bring to developing countries may be capital intensive and create little employment.

[Paragraph 4]

The potential costs and benefits of foreign direct investment imply that developing countries may need to restrict and regulate the entry and operations of MNCs.

(Source: adapted from Suneja, V., 2000, B200 *Markets Module 2 Study Guide*, Milton Keynes, The Open University)

Text 6.2

The advantages of MNC investment for the host state

[Paragraph 1]

Host governments are always on the look-out to attract foreign direct investment, and are prepared to put up considerable finance and make significant concessions to attract overseas business. So what benefits do MNCs bring to the economy?

[Paragraph 2]

Employment

MNCs clearly bring investment (even if much of the fixed cost is met by the host nation) and this constitutes a stimulus to economic activity and employment creation. As is the case with the UK, most countries attempt to entice MNCs to depressed regions where investment is low and unemployment is high. Often these will be regions where a major industry has closed (e.g. the coal-mining regions of South Wales). The employment that MNCs create is both direct, in the form of people employed in the new production facility, and indirect, through the impact that the MNC has on the local economy. This might be the consequence of establishing a new supply network, or simply the result of the increase in local incomes and expenditure, and hence the stimulus to local business.

[Paragraph 3]

Recent UK government estimates suggest that since 1979 some 800 000 jobs have been either created or saved by foreign investment. Such estimates are, however, very difficult to confirm, given the detrimental impact that MNC investment might have on domestic producers. For example, jobs created in one region of a country by a new MNC venture, with its superior technology and working practices, might cause a business to fold elsewhere, thus leading to increased unemployment in that region. Nationally the level of unemployment may remain the same: all that has changed is its geographical location.

[Paragraph 4]

The employment-generating effects of MNC investment will also be limited if the investment simply involves the purchase of existing producers, and does not involve the establishment of a new production facility. Thus we need to identify the nature of MNC involvement in the economy in order to estimate its potential employment effects.

[Paragraph 5]

The balance of payments

A country's balance of payments is likely to improve as a result of inward MNC investment, the investment representing a direct flow of capital into the country.

[Paragraph 6]

The beneficial effect on the balance of payments, however, will be offset to the extent that profits earned from the investment are repatriated to the parent country, and to the extent that the exports of the MNC displace the exports of domestic producers.

[Paragraph 7]

In the UK it is estimated that around half of all output produced by overseas-owned manufacturers is exported. The effect of inward investment represents a positive contribution to the UK balance of payments of about £700 million a year.

[Paragraph 8]

Technology transfer

Technology transfer refers to the benefits gained by domestic producers from the technology imported by the MNC. Such benefits can occur in a number of ways. The most common is where domestic producers copy the production technology and working practices of the MNC. This is referred to as the 'demonstration effect' and has occurred widely in the UK as British businesses have attempted to emulate many of the practices brought into the country by Japanese multinationals.

[Paragraph 9]

In addition to copying best practice, technology might also be transferred through the training of workers. When workers move jobs from the MNC to other firms in the industry, or to other industrial sectors, they take their newly acquired technical knowledge and skills with them.

[Paragraph 10]

Taxation

MNCs, like domestic producers, are required to pay tax and therefore contribute to public finances. Given the highly profitable nature of many MNCs, the level of tax revenue raised from this source could be highly significant.

The disadvantages of MNC investment for the host state

[Paragraph 11]

Thus far we have focused on the positive effects resulting from multinational investment. However, multinational investment may not always be beneficial in either the short or the long term. We have already noted that the repatriation of profits might effectively undermine many or all of the potential gains from multinational investment. In addition to these concerns, we might identify the following.

[Paragraph 12]

Uncertainty

MNCs are often 'footloose', meaning that they can simply close down their operations in foreign countries and move. This is especially likely with older plants which would need updating if the MNC were to remain, or with plants that can be easily sold without too much loss. The ability to close down its business operations and shift production, while being a distinct economic advantage to the MNC, is a prime concern facing the host nation. If a country has a large foreign multinational sector within the economy, it will become very vulnerable to such footloose activity, and face great uncertainty in the long term. It may thus be forced to offer the multinational 'perks' (e.g. grants, special tax relief or specific facilities) in order to persuade it to remain. These perks are clearly costly to the taxpayer.

[Paragraph 13]

Control

The fact that an MNC can shift production locations not only gives it economic flexibility, but enables it to exert various controls over its host. This is particularly so in many developing countries, where MNCs are not only major employers but in many cases the principal wealth creators. Thus attempts by the host state to, for example, improve worker safety or impose pollution controls may be against what the MNC sees as its own best interests. It might thus oppose such measures or even threaten to withdraw from the country if such measures are not modified or dropped. The host nation is in a very weak position.

[Paragraph 14]

MNCs, like domestic producers, are always attempting to reduce their tax liabilities. One unique way that an MNC can do this is through a process known as 'transfer pricing'. This enables the MNC to reduce its profits in countries with high rates of profit tax, and increase them in countries with low rates of profit tax.

[Paragraph 15]

This can be achieved by simply manipulating its internal pricing structure. For example, take a vertically integrated MNC where subsidiary A in one country supplies components to subsidiary B in another. The price at which the components are transferred between the two subsidiaries will ultimately determine the costs and hence the levels of profit made in each country. Assume that in the country where subsidiary A is located, the level of corporation tax is half that of the country where subsidiary B is located. If components are transferred from A to B at very high prices, then B's costs will rise and its profitability will fall. Conversely, A's profitability will rise. The MNC clearly benefits as more profit is taxed at the lower rather than the higher rate. Had it been the other way round, with subsidiary B facing the lower rate of tax, then the components would be transferred at a low price. This would increase subsidiary B's profits and reduce A's.

[Paragraph 16]

The practice of transfer pricing has reached such a level in the USA that, according to recent estimates, the federal government is losing some US$125 million per day in tax revenue. The extent of this tax evasion was revealed when it was found that a US-based multinational subsidiary purchased toothbrushes from an affiliate for a price of US$18 each!

[Paragraph 17]

The environment

Many MNCs are accused of simply investing in countries to gain access to natural resources, which are subsequently extracted or used in a way that is not sensitive to the environment. Host nations, especially developing countries, that are keen for investment are frequently prepared to allow MNCs to do this. They often put more store on the short-run gains from the MNC's presence than on the long-run depletion of precious natural resources or damage to the environment. Governments, like many businesses, often have a very short-run focus: they are concerned more with their political survival (whether through the ballot box or through military force) than with the long-term interests of people.

(Source: adapted from Suneja, V. (ed.), 2000, *Understanding Business: Markets*, Milton Keynes, The Open University, pp. 204–8)

Text 6.3

News article about Asda

i usually go to Tesco but i came here for the chicken mrs walmsley said standing near the poultry counter its a giveaway everything is going up in price so every day now we only eat chicken the chicken she was after was pale and not particularly appetising but one look at the label explained why she had made her special trip it weighed 1.5kg was British and fresh and cost just £2 mrs walmsleys most difficult choice was whether to buy two or three she took three asda and tesco are waging a price war and along with Harry Potter books and school uniforms chicken is on the frontline Asda boasts that its

£2 chicken is now iconic one of the few foods that people will cross town for the miserable summer has more than made up for the loss of trade in barbecues, says rachel fellows a spokeswoman for the store the more people stay indoors the more they eat chicken it sometimes seems as though the super competitive stores are using chicken to snipe at each other just for the sake of it if Tesco reduces the price of its healthy frozen skinless chicken breast by a penny one week asda will follow suit the next i don't know how the supermarkets can sell it for £2 says Nigel Joice regional chairman of the national farmers unions poultry board who has invested millions of pounds to rear 880000 broiler chickens a year on a modern farm in north Norfolk he sells broiler eating chickens to most supermarket but declines to say which we are not losing money on the £2 bird fellows said the price works for the consumer and also the supplier who wants to sell large volumes but she adds they meet us part of the way which is asdas way of saying that the £2 chicken wars are driving down the prices paid to farmers

(Source: adapted from *The Guardian*, 2007)

Acknowledgements

Grateful acknowledgement is made to the following source:

Text

Pages 32–35, Text 5.2, Text 6.2: Sloman, J. and Sutcliffe, M. (1998) *Economics for Business*, Pearson Education Ltd, © John Sloman and Mark Sutcliffe 1998 © Pearson Education 2001.